THERE WAS
A TIME

PRECEDING PAGES:

Coastal kampong, Pulau Ubin, c 1960. In the 1960s, the island had a population of 2,000, three-quarters of whom were Chinese, a quarter Malay and the remaining Indians. "Ubin" is Malay for granite, and quarries on the island which supplied stone for the building of Horsburgh Lighthouse, Fort Canning and the Causeway operated from the mid-1840s till the 1960s.

Housing Development Board estate, 1965. The HDB, established in 1960, not only addressed the post-war housing shortage, but its masterplans also included public spaces and facilities, such as playgrounds, markets and schools.

The waterfront skyline, c 1959. From left: Ocean Building topped with its lantern, Alkaff Arcade with its Moorish façade, the 15-storey Shell House, Union Building, Hongkong and Shanghai Bank Building, and Fullerton Building.

Published by
Landmark Books Pte Ltd
5001 Beach Road, #02-73/74, Singapore 199588

Supported by the National Archives of Singapore

The National Archives of Singapore – an institution of the National Library Board – is the official keeper of Singapore's history and heritage, and is responsible for the collection, preservation and management of the nation's public and private archival records. (www.nas.gov.sg)

ISBN 978-981-14-6795-0
Printed by KHL Printing Co Pte Ltd

THERE WAS A TIME

Singapore from Self-Rule to Independence
1959-1965

·LANDM△RK·BOOKS·

SUPPORTED BY

NATIONAL
ARCHIVES
OF SINGAPORE

An institution of the National Library Board

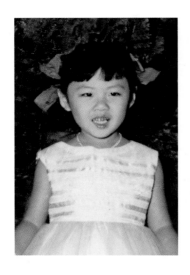

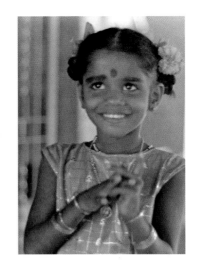

PUBLISHER'S PREFACE

The title of this book is the opening phrase of *We Are Singapore*, the National Day song of 1987: "There was a time when people said that Singapore won't make it, but we did."

The images on these pages show what Singapore was like between 1959 and 1965; that is from when the country was granted internal self-rule by the colonial British to the year it became a sovereign nation. This was the time when naysayers doubted Singapore's ability to manage its internal affairs, much less survive as an independent country.

But in this period, Singapore began its process of change as it progressed from being another one of Britain's colonies to a nation in its own right.

The intention of this book is to portray the rhythms of daily life during this pivotal time. Photographs from government and private collections in the National Archives of Singapore, as well as others from personal albums, were chosen and arranged to show morning, afternoon and night-time activities. Political actions – riots, elections and insurgency, as well as extraordinary events such as the Bukit Ho Swee fire of 1961, although represented in the Introduction – were intentionally omitted from the main part of the book.

Among the photographers known and unknown whose 328 works appear here, Wong Ken Foo or K.F. Wong, a prize-winning and acclaimed photographer, and his 83 images, deserve special mention. The K.F. Wong Collection in the National Archives comprises over 2,000 photographs. Mostly depicting Singapore between 1945 and 1966, many are street scenes that capture the small but expressive moments of daily life.

The context to the album is given by Lee Geok Boi who has written on many fields of Singapore history. In her Introduction, she mines her memories as a teenager during this period and skilfully weaves them into social history.

Children of Singapore who saw the country develop and change.

This was a time when kampong folk moved up to high-rise blocks, when new jobs came with the factories built in Jurong. Ethnic costumes as everyday wear were changing to Western styles. Schools integrating students of different races were founded. The Primary Production Department was formed to help farmers provide more food from land and sea. The trading of stocks and shares began. The red-brick National Library opened on Stamford Road. Television came to Singapore. It was a time when Singaporeans welcomed change.

But it was not all shifting scenes. The Singapore River remained a working waterway and bumboats, its muscle. Families – mostly large then – strolled along Queen Elizabeth Walk to catch the sea breeze. People gossiped in corner coffee shops and ate street-side at hawker stalls. Children amused themselves in found spaces and five-foot-ways. The skyline of the city was largely low-rise and enjoyed an old-world elegance.

Readers who remember the scenes in this book will recall them with fond nostalgia. Those who do not will have a view of that simpler, unhurried life.

GROWING TOWARDS INDEPENDENCE
by Lee Geok Boi

It was 1959 – a year of huge change for Singapore society, and for me. I was 12 going on 13 in June, the same month that Singapore became self-governing, 140 years after Sir Stamford Raffles established a trading post here that would eventually turn the island into a British colony.

To mark the occasion and to encourage a sense of loyalty among the diverse citizens of the new state of Singapore, National Solidarity Week was organised in December. A mass drill by schoolchildren was one of the planned events. I can still remember the heat of the sun beating down on me as I, together with rows and rows of other schoolgirls, went through the routines on the little field of my convent school in the sticks of Upper Serangoon.

I have absolutely no memory of being at the actual event though. A former classmate told me that the performance was held on the field of St Joseph's Institution in Bras Basah Road; she remembered the occasion because she had fainted. Perhaps I fell ill and had to stay home?

The year when Singapore became self-governing and the People's Action Party (PAP) won its first general election marked the beginning of the transformation of Singapore from a colonial port into a global city-state.

Singapore in 1959 was no fishing village. It had already an established international profile as an exotic destination. Hollywood released a movie in 1940 titled *The Road to Singapore* that featured Bob Hope, and 'Singapore' as a fantasy destination popped up in popular songs like the 1939 'On a Little Street in Singapore' memorably recorded by Frank Sinatra, and Eve Boswell's 'Moon Over Malaya' in 1953.

Polling for the Legislative Assembly General Election, 30 May 1959.

By the 1950s, constitutional changes and citizenship registration had created a sharply divided electorate that picked a group of politicians who were committed to improving the lives of the residents of Singapore, and who had the actual economic and political savvy to execute this agenda.

The fight against communism
Getting elected, however, was by no means an easy political process for the PAP. Singapore at the time was a society riven by political ideologies. The immediate post-war years had seen the rise of the Malayan Communist Party and the sparking of the guerrilla war in Malaya that was euphemistically called the Emergency. (Calling it a war would have made insurance for the rubber plantations – the bulwark of the Malayan and Singapore economy – very expensive.)

In Singapore, this Malayan guerrilla war manifested itself in restive Chinese schools and communist-infiltrated trade unions. The trade union leaders were constantly in search of reasons to go on strike and the politically active Chinese middle schools students were equally agitated, attracted to the communist agenda of the People's Republic of China that had emerged in 1949.

One day in 1956, the year my family moved to Serangoon Garden Estate,

Chinese High School examination boycott, 15 May 1962.

rioting Chinese middle-school students prevented me from going to school. I still have the vivid memory of standing in the garden of our new home watching a military helicopter hovering overhead with loudhailers warning people to get off the streets because of the curfew.

The Singapore Chinese community then was deeply divided. Even as a schoolgirl, I was aware of the schism between the English-educated and the Chinese-educated. In 1959, the number of students who went to Chinese primary schools and those who went to English primary schools was nearly equal.

In my convent-blue uniform, I was easily identified as English-educated. Labels such as 'running dog of imperialism', a left-wing taunt, or the Hokkien phrase that translates into 'eating the turd of the Europeans' were sometimes spewed by the more militant Chinese youths. This division was in part created by a colonial-era education system that had left the schools free to choose their medium of instruction, resulting in English-stream, Chinese-stream, Malay-stream and Tamil-stream schools.

This vernacular educational divide was as much fuelled by significant differences in economic opportunities and employment rates as ideological differences and political dynamics. Navigating this terrain required smart moves on the part of the PAP leadership.

The PAP had been formed in 1957 as a multiracial party – a key feature that became a critical issue between 16 September 1963 and 9 August 1965 when, as part of Malaysia, Singapore faced tensions arising from attempts by race-based political parties in Kuala Lumpur to meddle with Singapore's race dynamics.

In 1959, the PAP was led by English-educated moderates who had to court the favour of the Chinese-educated who formed the majority of the Chinese community in Singapore.

English-educated political leaders like Lee Kuan Yew and Dr Goh Keng Swee were more acceptable to the British colonial government than Chinese-educated leaders like Lim Chin Siong and Fong Swee Suan, two left-leaning trade unionists who have been described as pro-communists in historical accounts of the tussle for political power at this time. But without the support of the Chinese-educated, whether left-leaning or not, the moderates in the PAP stood little chance of gaining the popular vote.

This alliance between the English-educated and the Chinese-educated in the PAP leadership made conservative English-educated families like mine uneasy. This discomfiture would be exacerbated when the newly elected PAP government slashed the salaries of civil servants to balance the public books.

My father found ends so hard to meet that he took in a couple of lodgers for a number of years until the pay cuts were restored when the economy began improving. It was only when the more centrist political positions of Lee Kuan Yew became clearer and Dr Goh Keng Swee's economic reforms began to kick in that my father became a fervent PAP supporter.

A slice of middle-class life

The severe housing shortage in the 1950s, a consequence of the Japanese Occupation and the post-war baby boom, would be addressed with the formation of the Housing and Development Board in 1960 and the start of its home-building programme soon after. But before public housing was ready, the shortage was addressed by sharing homes with related or even unrelated families and by the Rent Control Act that prevented landlords from evicting tenants for higher rents.

Protesting workers in a labour union office, 10 August 1963.

My grandparents and parents had shared a large, pre-war, rent-controlled bungalow in Palm Grove Avenue in Serangoon with two unrelated families as well as two single aunts from Kuala Lumpur who had come to Singapore for work. When my grandmother passed away, my grandfather helped my father to put down the deposit for a loan from the government-sponsored Thrift and Loan Society to buy a house in Serangoon Garden Estate.

In 1956, the three-room house in Chartwell Drive was shared by 10 people: my immediate family of five, my grandfather, an aunt's family of three, and a maid. The aunt's family had the biggest room; my parents had the middle room while my grandfather and us three children shared the smallest room at the back of the house. The children slept three-across in a double bed and Grandfather had a corner of his own that was screened off from us by a large, sturdy clothes rack on which we hung our clothes, towels and odds and ends. The live-in maid slept on the floor of the spacious living room, moving her bedding in and out daily.

Despite this, our circumstances were decidedly middle-class, a relatively small economic layer made up mostly of English-educated Asians of different races working in the civil service, and as professionals and managers in British, European or Chinese companies. The wealthy layer above the middle class comprised mostly of Chinese business people, of whom many were Chinese-educated but whose ranks also included the Straits Chinese or the Babas.

My grandfather was a Baba who had migrated to Singapore from Kuching. He had become a certificated accountant by dint of on-the-job training and night school and he worked for a Chinese import-export company that did well given Singapore's thriving entrepôt trade.

Although not in the class of old money, Grandfather certainly earned enough to bet on horses and indulge in luxury soaps and hair oils as well as imported tinned and bottled food. Chinese New Year staples that he enjoyed included a leg of ham, brandy and beer.

My father, on the other hand, was a humble civil servant without expensive Anglophile tastes. He was a certified interpreter, a job he secured in 1949. Typical of many Straits Chinese families, he had gone to both Chinese and English schools and was linguistically gifted enough to become proficient in both languages. He could converse in Hakka to my grandmothers who were both Hakka, and also Hokkien. He picked up Teochew and Cantonese in the course of his work, as well as Malay.

He started with what was then a grand salary of $85 a month, boosted by various British civil service allowances he received. Grandfather, being generous with his earnings, made us effectively a two-income household. Unusual for that time, my aunt was a working woman (and one who smoked to boot); she too contributed to the household's expenses until she moved out. Thus, my father was able to maintain a second-hand Baby Austin, make mortgage payments on the house, as well as look after a family of five.

With the exception of my mother – who spoke her mother tongue of Hakka, Hokkien and Malay – all of us spoke English at home. Speaking English was the norm in many English-educated homes, particularly among Straits Chinese and Indian families. The Malay family of nine next door to us spoke mostly Malay at home although the younger folks tended also to converse in English among themselves and with us.

The differences in society created by different educational backgrounds would never be so stark again, as following self-government in 1959 and in-

The author's relatives from Kuala Lumpur on Jurong Hill to see the development of the industrial estate, c 1961.

Land survey by the Housing and Development Board in preparation for the clearance of Toa Payoh Village, 1963.

dependence in 1965, the education system was slowly reformed to create a Singaporean society. English became the medium of instruction for all schools and vernacular schools disappeared.

Serangoon district and Serangoon Garden Estate

Serangoon Garden Estate, which was subsequently renamed Serangoon Gardens, was one of the earliest middle-class housing estates in Singapore. In the 1950s, Serangoon was a rural district dotted with numerous villages. Our house was in Chartwell Drive, and right behind it was a village of attap houses, rubber trees and even a rubber smokehouse that we could smell when the wind blew in our direction.

About half an hour's walk uphill from my home was a small kampong along a dirt road that has since become Jalan Nira. At the other border of the housing estate was Kampung Cheng San. Along Yio Chu Kang Road, one of the two main roads into Serangoon Gardens, was Chia Keng Village. The other access road was Lorong Chuan that led to Braddell Road. At this junction, if you turned left, you were heading towards Upper Serangoon Road; if you turned right you were going to Toa Payoh which, in the 1950s, consisted of squatter villages.

One of the first major tasks of the newly set-up Housing and Development Board was to clear these squatter villages to make way for blocks of public housing with modern conveniences. Given the contentious politics of the time, clearing squatter villages was a complex business even if few villages had piped water, electricity or indoor plumbing.

If the village had an entrepreneur with enough cash, he bought a generator and sold electricity to his neighbours. Villages had wells and one of the first moves by the new government to improve the lives of the villagers was to introduce water standpipes.

Vegetable farms lined Braddell Road. From this village of vegetable farmers would, in 1973, come the 16-year-old girl named Ah Moey (meaning Little

Sister) who would work for me as a domestic helper and mind my young children. She would subsequently leave in the mid-1970s to work in a factory. By then, factory jobs were plentiful and life as a factory hand was more interesting than as a domestic worker. When the family first moved to Serangoon Gardens, my mother's live-in maid, Ah Choot, had come from a similar village near Boon Keng Road. Ah Choot left us around 1960 to marry a young man from Jalan Nira. Ah Choot remained in the neighbourhood after her marriage, eventually finding better paying employment as a daily maid for a British family in the neighbourhood.

Ah Choot's husband was a tinsmith with a small workshop in the village. Taking a walk to watch him at work was a simple treat during my school holidays. He made buckets, dust pans, funnels, watering cans and bath tubs (those were the days before plastic products) and eventually aluminium baking tins and cookie sheets, some of which I still use today. The village had a large pond where rafts of ducks paddled and feasted on a lush carpeting of duckweed and water hyacinth with beautiful purple flowers.

Serangoon Garden Estate was built in the 1950s to house officers of the British forces based in Singapore. The whole area was therefore heavily dependent on their patronage, and Britain's decision in 1967 to close the Singapore military base struck fear in businesses, and in the maids and base personnel who depended on the presence of the British for their livelihood.

The well-known circus of Serangoon Garden Estate, 1965.

The British families shaped the shopping area in Serangoon Gardens, which consisted of several rows of single-storied shophouses next to the traffic roundabout named Serangoon Gardens Circus. My favourite shop was a general store that stocked books and imported magazines, candy, stationery and knick-knacks. There was a second-hand bookstall where you could exchange two books for one or pay between 50 cents and a dollar for a book depending on its condition.

For me, one of the benefits of living in a British forces enclave came in the form of discarded newspapers. These were my early access to good writing. The British family who lived next door took to giving me copies of their imported newspapers after they were done with them. The tabloid came stapled together into a thick volume between bright-yellow covers. One columnist whom I enjoyed reading went by the name 'Cassandra' which I later learnt was the pen name for William Connor of *The Daily Mirror*, a journalist noted for his acerbic prose!

Food for all

There were at least two grocery stores in Serangoon Gardens selling British staples such as Wall's tinned sausages, Heinz baked beans, frozen lamb and beef, and Birds Eye fish fingers. There were restaurants that served steaks and chops, pubs with beer on tap, and cafés with a large selection of iced cakes and meat pies. A fish and chips shop here also sent a van round the neighbourhood in the evenings to drum up business.

Asians never stepped foot into the air-conditioned restaurants or cafés patronised by the British families, although I was bold enough to sometimes pop in to get a meat pie or a sugary iced cake for a treat or a special occasion. One such time was when I organised a little birthday party – for whom I cannot

remember – to which several school friends living in the estate were invited for tea, cakes, bananas and cordial.

Serangoon Gardens election victory celebration dinner at Sin Hwa School, Lim Tua Tow Road, 8 September 1963.

Where food was concerned, the Asians in the estate were by no means bereft of choice. The coffee shop opposite my home had stalls selling Indian curry rice, Hokkien *mee*, and, of course, chicken rice. Itinerant hawkers roamed the estate, ringing bells or striking bamboo clappers to announce their presence at your door.

There was the *rojak* man who scooped his offering into cones of freshly cut Simpoh Air leaves held together with a toothpick. The *chye tau kueh* man came on a large tricycle equipped with a burning stove, turning out a sweet black soya sauce-coated radish cake cut into large cubes. The *char kuay tiao* hawker showed up in the late afternoon.

In the early 1960s, these itinerant hawkers would form themselves into a makeshift hawker centre around the bus stop – the origin of the famous Chomp Chomp across the road from where they gathered.

Among the itinerant hawkers who plied their wares on the streets in the 1960s were those who sold household goods such as brooms made of coconut leaf ribs and coir, feather dusters, bamboo poles and aluminium buckets. A soya sauce maker, who was always dressed in an indigo Chinese-style jacket, came around with large jars of sauces arranged on the flatbed of his tricycle. Customers had to bring their own containers for what they bought.

At night, there was a hawker who sold snacks such as *kana-kana* (preserved fruits) and groundnuts, also from a tricycle. His goods would be illuminated by carbide lamps which, along with kerosene pressure lamps, were very common forms of lighting at that time.

A favourite after-dinner activity, particularly among the women and children, was to sit in the garden in semi-darkness to snack on *kana* and nuts and listen to the elders gossip or tell stories. I have no memory of being bitten by mosquitoes, only of the voices of my mother and my aunt, the taste of peanuts, the cool evening, and the glow of stars in the dark night sky.

Eating out was a monthly treat on pay day when my father drove us to Koek Road for *satay chelop* and *ice kacang*. Occasionally, he brought home hawker fare we'd never seen before. One was the white *chye tau kueh* which was introduced in the 1960s by an innovative hawker in Chinatown. The standard fried radish cake at that time was coated with sweet black sauce and dressed with garlic and chilli sauce. Then there was the occasional packet of fried Hokkien *mee* wrapped in *opeh*, the palm leaf sheath. It was known as Rochor *mee* then because a hawker in the area around Seventh Storey Hotel came up with this dish.

My grandfather was the other source of food treats. A typical Baba, he enjoyed all-night mahjong sessions which took place at the home of a Baba *kaki* (friend) living in Devonshire Road, which was not far from Killiney Road where Teck Kee, a *pao* shop famous for its *char siew pao*, was located. Whenever I spotted *char siew pao* for breakfast on the kitchen table, I knew he had some winnings and that was the time to ask him for cash to buy a book or a bar of chocolate. Once, I asked him for money to go to the hairdressing salon to cut off my long hair. Audrey Hepburn's boyish haircut in *Roman Holiday* may have been the rage then but my conservative mother did not approve of short hair for girls.

Mobile hawker stalls in Woodlands, 1965.

Another treat from my grandfather was *nasi biryani* from Islamic, a popular Indian-Muslim restaurant in North Bridge Road, and one of the restaurants he favoured. Fatty's in Albert Street was another restaurant which he liked, so after taking the grandchildren to the movies, we invariably went to Fatty's for dinner. Fatty was a jolly, round Cantonese man who spoke a smattering of English because his roadside stall (what we would call a *zhi char* stall today) was popular with the British forces.

Seating was on both floors of the shophouse behind the stall, and my favourite table was the one next to the window with a view of the cook busily stir-frying away. Fatty did classic Cantonese dishes such as sweet and sour pork, stewed ribs in black bean sauce, roast duck and *char siew*. An added dinner treat was soda pop: Green Spot or Red Lion, two still orange drinks that seem to have disappeared. Soft drinks were only offered to children on such occasions and at festivals like Chinese New Year.

Treats were relatively simple in the 1950s and 60s. During school holidays, besides visiting the tinsmith at the Jalan Nira village, we also walked to Kampung Cheng San to visit our washerwoman's family. Hor Keow Sim, her pirate-taxi-driver husband and their five or six children lived in an attap house with an earthen floor.

In her relatively spacious kitchen sat a wood-fired stove on which rested a huge wok with which she cooked swill for the few pigs that she kept in a sty in the compound. She also reared chickens, collecting their eggs for sale. The papayas, limes and *binjai* fruit that grew around the house were also regularly harvested and sold. We were often given the fruits in exchange for the food scraps for swill that her son would regularly collect from us.

In the 1960s, before the proliferation of washing machines, many women from the rural areas made a living as washerwomen, and Hor Keow Sim did washing and ironing for several families in Serangoon Gardens to supplement the household income.

Her husband, the pirate taxi driver, drove an old black saloon, ferrying well-off children to school. There were no school buses then and you either walked, used the public bus or such pirate taxis. Naturally, he would pack as many children as he could into the car, making several trips in the mornings and afternoons, which meant that if you couldn't fit into the first load, you had to wait for the next trip. I made one of my best friends when we were squashed together while travelling to and from school! However, when I turned 14, I begged to take the 10-cent public bus ride to school instead.

My school, St Joseph's Convent in Hillside Drive, drew girls from rural Serangoon. Some schoolmates came from landed properties in Rosyth Road, Highland Road, Simon Road, Flower Road and Palm Grove Avenue, areas which then consisted of a mix of bungalows and clumps of attap houses.

There were also girls who came from Punggol and Kangkar, coastal areas that were populated by Teochew fishermen. Inland was Au Kang (later Hougang in Hanyu Pinyin) which was Teochew for 'Port at the Back'. As many Teochews lived in these areas, my school had a high proportion of Teochew speakers.

A picnic organised by east-coast community centres at Tanah Merah Youth Camp, 1960.

Entertainment and weekend outings

For entertainment, there was the radio with music and different language programmes. My favourites were the stories from the BBC, the best loved of which were about Paul Temple, a debonair writer and amateur sleuth with a glamorous wife nicknamed Steve! There was also Rediffusion, a private cable radio station that also broadcast dialect programmes, the most famous of which were the stories told by Lee Dai Soh.

Every coffee shop, including the one opposite my Chartwell Drive home, had a boxy Rediffusion set that was turned on all day long. This coffee shop also had a juke box and occasionally a patron would pop in a coin and choose his favourite song. A perennial favourite was Johnny Mathis' 'Chances Are'.

Cinemas like Capitol, Cathay and Odeon were in town but Serangoon Gardens Country Club did have open-air screenings of popular movies once a week. The patrons brought their own snacks, mats and pillows to stretch out on the basketball court to watch the film. I caught *Seven Brides for Seven Brothers* and *Calamity Jane* under the stars this way. The open-air film screenings were replaced by television when it was introduced to Singapore in 1963. My father got us our own set. If I recall rightly, it was made in Germany, either a Grundig or Telefunken? Japanese TV sets were unheard of at that time. Thus, I saw for myself in real time that iconic footage of Prime Minister Lee Kuan Yew in tears when announcing Singapore's exit from the Federation of Malaysia.

I had, from a very early age, a membership in the Raffles Library which was then part of the Raffles Library and Museum. While my father never bought us toys, he loved books and always went to the trouble of regularly borrowing books for us. During the school holidays, my father would drop me and my siblings at the library on a Saturday morning while he went off to work, showing up again at 1 pm to take us to lunch.

The children's library was in the building right opposite a huge banyan tree

The Trekkers, a Singapore boy band of the 1960s.

that stood at the corner of the driveway into the Raffles Museum grounds. Under the banyan tree was an Indian *ice kacang* man who sold ice balls for 10 cents a piece, 20 cents if you wanted red beans enclosed within. We would sit and read in the library for as long as we wanted, then go off to get an ice ball. We also spent time in the museum.

Despite having free admission, the museum attracted very few people even on a Saturday and we kids had the run of the place. The exhibits looked every bit as old as the museum. Above a staircase was a complete set of whale bones that hung suspended from the ceiling. Another room had lines of covered display cases. Lift a canvas cover and you would see row upon row of butterflies, moths, insects and other creepy crawlies pinned down in the dimmed recesses.

In one corner of the top floor was a short metal spiral staircase leading to the roof. A story circulated that it really led to a haunted room. We always went to that staircase to look at the chain across the bottom step and the door above, enjoying the shivers at the thought of what we might see if we sneaked up. We never did.

At lunchtime came one of the best parts of our Saturday outing to the library – lunch at Waterloo Street. Here were found several Indian food hawkers. One stall had the best *mee goreng* in Singapore, the other the best Indian *rojak*. The third was a drinks stall where the choice for many was pink *susu bandung* with a dollop of finely chopped *chin chao*. This was the only place I have ever found such a combination. In the 1960s, the number of Indian hawker stalls along that stretch of Waterloo Street multiplied but with the 1980s urban renewal, these street hawkers disappeared into modern food centres. Ever since, *mee goreng* has never been the same or as tasty.

Other outings were Sunday picnics of chicken curry and bread on Changi Beach, evening drives simply to *makan angin* (literally 'eat the wind') or strolling down the Esplanade and stopping for an ice-cream, lollipop or *kacang puteh* bought from the hawkers who clustered there.

There was an open-air food centre at the Singapore Recreation Club end of the Esplanade that served only dinner because eating lunch while seated on the metal chairs provided would have been too uncomfortable. The best thing that I can remember eating here was the *ice kacang*.

Another kind of outing that I enjoyed was going to the wet market with my mother. There, I watched the fish ball man beat fish paste by hand and the Indian spice woman prepare freshly ground spices and blend them according to your needs. For a larger selection of produce, my mother went to Lim Tua Tow Market at Fifth Mile, Upper Serangoon Road, and more rarely, the Sixth Mile Market where the seafood was believed to be of better quality because the market was nearer to Kangkar where the fishermen docked.

Before shopping at Lim Tua Tow Market, breakfast was always fish ball noodles from a coffee shop where it was said the stallholder made his own noodles and fish balls. It was likely that he made his own sauces too, for this was the era before mass manufacturing led to standardised flavours everywhere.

My mother believed in shopping for fresh food daily. Although my grandfather had bought her a refrigerator when we moved to Serangoon Gardens, she never cared for the convenience of frozen food until late in life when daily walks to the wet market became onerous.

Browsing for books in the Reading Room of the National Library, 1961.

Mother bought provisions from a Chinese grocery shop in the shophouses near the traffic roundabout in Serangoon Gardens. She used the chit system, the credit scheme found in British colonies everywhere: purchases were recorded in a notebook on credit and payment made on pay day. If she ran short of something during the month, one of us kids would be sent to the shop armed only with this booklet, never cash. The monthly groceries were always delivered to the house.

The shopkeeper started with a bicycle and eventually upgraded to a small car and then a van. The chit system and home deliveries disappeared with the advent of supermarkets although this provision shop continued to deliver groceries to my parents even after they moved out of Serangoon Gardens. In 2014, the elderly widow of the man who ran this provision shop called my father to announce that she was closing the business as none of her children wanted to take it over and also because it was no longer viable given the plethora of supermarkets.

Clothing, fashion and shopping

One of the long-gone features of life in the 1960s was homemade clothes. Even the first First Lady of Singapore, Toh Puan Noor Aishah, the wife of the first President of Singapore, Yusof Ishak, said that she made her own *kebaya*.

Mother sewed her own samfoos, our clothes and school uniforms but her *kebaya* were sewn and embroidered at a shop in Geylang, and my father's work clothes were made by a professional tailor.

Shopping for cloth was fun. Off we'd go to S. A. Majeed in High Street to get the convent-blue fabric for uniforms. The treat on this outing was always lunch at a well-known coffee shop in Hock Lam Street. For Chinese New Year, we would buy cloth for clothes at textile shops near Lim Tua Tow Market.

I wore homemade clothes as an undergraduate in the 1960s, right up till the start of my working life in 1969. I even learnt to sew clothes from my mother. And if you could not sew, there was a cottage industry of women who took in sewing jobs for a living. One of such women was an aunt who lived in Bukit Ho Swee, a slum area that would burn down spectacularly in 1961 in one of Singapore's biggest fires.

The shopping areas downtown were Raffles Place, Orchard Road and the High Street-North Bridge Road nexus. Robinsons was in Raffles Place but someone like my mother was too intimidated by the British presence to consider stepping in there. (I did though when pre-university school friends discovered apple pie à la mode at the Robinsons café.)

Orchard Road was known for C K Tang and Antoinette, to which I went but once in 1962 with an Anglo-Chinese pre-university classmate to get a school belt in fashionable patent leather.

High Street had a very popular department store named Aurora. Also in High Street was Wassiamull that sold imported clothing. One day in 1964, I found a pair of off-white imported Lee jeans at a discount. It was my very first pair of jeans and I wore it to lectures the next day, to the surprise of some of my fellow undergraduates since even the boys did not wear jeans but trousers. At the time, women wore dresses to lectures and indeed, everywhere else. Many Indian girls on campus wore the sari.

The author (extreme left) and her sister dressed in the height of fashion – homemade empire-line dresses with skirts puffed up with can-can petticoats, 1962.

Working women all wore dresses; trousers or pant suits were rare indeed, if unheard off. Even in the late 1960s, women wore only dresses to work. As I recall, I got around the unwritten rule in the early 1970s by wearing the *seluar kamis* as I was very comfortable wearing ethnic clothing. I wore the *sarong kebaya*, *baju kurong*, sari and cheongsam too on occasion. Managers went about in tie and jacket, and even clerks put on a tie and long-sleeved shirt.

In the 1950s and 60s, the formal wear was the cheongsam for Chinese women, the *sarong kebaya* for Malay women and the sari for Indian women. Casual wear for girls and women were dresses although traditional Chinese women wore the samfoo. In my convent school, the girls doing PE wore the uniform blouse over baggy bloomers. Shorts for women were unheard of. Only labourers wore shorts and singlets at work.

The great Bukit Ho Swee fire and its aftermath, 1961.

Education

In 1959, my French convent school switched from offering French as a second language to having all the students learn Malay, although Chinese was also a choice. In 1961, when I reached my Senior Cambridge O-levels, my Malay teacher said she did not think I was good enough in Malay to pass it and so I dropped the second language. At the same time, my Mathematics teacher told me that I was not good enough to pass the subject at O-levels, so I dropped Maths too. To have enough subject groups to get a complete O-level certificate, I took up Art and Health Science in place of Malay and Maths.

I rather fancied the idea of going to work after my Senior Cambridge. However, at 15, I was not really legally employable. Most of my classmates were at least 17 and went on to become teachers and nurses.

I had gotten way ahead of the children of my age because I had started formal schooling at age 6 and ended up meeting older classmates who had had an extra year of primary school. They had gone through Primary 1 and Primary 2 before getting to Standard 1 and upwards to Standard 7, getting caught by the changes in the education system at that time.

I, on the other hand, had gone from Primary 1 to 4, and skipped over Primary 5 to go to Primary 6. A classmate from that year recalls that our cohort was the first to do a sort of primary school leaving examination or PSLE in 1957. It was certainly my first encounter with multiple-choice questions.

Secondary school started with Form 2 (Secondary 1 today) with the last year of secondary school being Form 5 (Secondary 4). Those who wanted higher education went on to Form 6 – Lower and Upper – which came to be called Pre-University 1 and 2.

The author (seated), her father, Lee Thian Leong (extreme right), and his friends, c 1959.

Family circumstances were often such that many girls could not afford to go for higher education. They had younger siblings to help look after. Those were the days before the government's Stop At Two family planning campaign which began in 1965. Culturally, too, many old-fashioned parents saw higher education for girls as a waste of time and money, given that girls were going to get married and become a member of another family's household. Out of my O-level class of 45, only a handful went on to pre-university, and from that handful, only two or three proceeded to university.

Another reason why many girls did not bother with higher education was that, armed with a Senior Cambridge School Certificate, they could find well-paying jobs as nurses and teachers, and with training in shorthand and typing, be in demand as clerks, secretaries, and even managers.

I had switched from the pre-university class in the Convent of the Holy Infant Jesus (CHIJ) on Victoria Street to Anglo-Chinese School because I decided that I had had enough of single-sex education. It was an independent decision in which my parents played no part. When my O-level results came out, I marched up Barker Road to apply for a place in a pre-university class there.

In my one term at CHIJ though, I became friends with some of the boys from St Joseph's Institution. One of them, Michael Khoo, occasionally held dance parties at his home in Goodman Road in the east coast area.

The Khoo family was unusual. Michael's father was an entertainer, a magician of note in Singapore, and Michael, too, picked up the skill and earned pocket money performing at Christmas and children's parties. His sister, Theresa, played the piano at a nightclub and his youngest brother, Victor, became a well-known ventriloquist who made frequent appearances on TV with a dummy named Charlie.

Michael's parties were always alcohol free and we all drank fruit punch and snacked on sandwiches, curry puffs and agar-agar. The focus really was on dancing: Rock and roll, waltz, foxtrot, quickstep and the cha cha cha. The two years of pre-university flew by and soon 1964 was upon me; it was time to head for university.

University life

In 1964, there were two universities and two polytechnics in Singapore. The Chinese-stream Nanyang University had been founded by Chinese philanthropists in 1953. A year later, the Singapore Polytechnic was founded, offering rather untechnical courses like embroidery and English Literature until Dr Toh Chin Chye became chairman of the board in 1959 and introduced a genuine technical curriculum with subjects like Engineering, Nautical Studies, Accountancy, and Building and Construction. The other polytechnic was Ngee Ann Polytechnic, started in 1963.

The fourth institution was the University of Singapore, which had started as the University of Malaya that was formed by the merger of the King Edward VII College of Medicine and Raffles College.

All university graduates looked to the civil service for jobs at that time. The general degree pay, even if you had passed with honours, started at $610 a month. That was what I was paid when I joined the library service in 1969 even though I had a Master's degree.

Despite an initial reluctance to continue studying after my O-levels, I discovered that I enjoyed not only the undergraduate life but also a life of discourse, arguments and analysis. And so I seized the opportunity to do a post-graduate degree when it was offered to me unexpectedly.

There were few takers for the Graduate Assistantship programme that allowed graduates to work on their post-graduate degrees with a $400 monthly subsidy from the university. Accepting this offer would have meant a loss of $210 a month, a considerable sum then. However, as my father did not need my financial support, I considered the $400 subsidy generous.

The years leading up to independence in 1965 were turbulent and event-filled in the universities, polytechnics and in Singapore. In the University of Singapore, the make-up of the University of Singapore Students' Union (USSU) mirrored the contention between left and right elements in the PAP that eventually led to the emergence of the Barisan Sosialis.

Security road block at North Bridge Road after the Prophet Mohamed Birthday race riots, July 1964.

USSU was part of a larger Singapore students' organisation that included the more left-leaning Nanyang University in Jurong as well as the students' unions of Singapore Polytechnic and Ngee Ann Polytechnic.

The University of Singapore Socialist Club was active in student politics and it once organised an anti-Vietnam War exhibition to protest the war. To counter the left-leaning Socialist Club, PAP supporters among the student population started the Democratic Socialist Club, and both political clubs constantly organised debates, forums and talks. In 1964, students were bold enough to protest the Kuala Lumpur government's implementation of the Suitability Certificate for all incoming university students that was designed to filter out student activism that had arisen in Nanyang University.

Outside the campuses, political strife began heating up as political leaders in Singapore and Kuala Lumpur exchanged increasingly hot words. On 21 July 1964, I found myself in a crush of people at Rex cinema where crowds were rushing home to beat the curfew that had been declared. Race riots had broken out in Kallang at a parade to celebrate Prophet Mohamed's birthday.

I had intended to watch a movie but seeing the chaos, decided that it would be safer to head back to the Bukit Timah campus than attempt to return home to Serangoon Gardens. Ironically, I was sheltered that night in Eusoffe College, the women's hostel in the university, by my best friend who was an Indian-Muslim girl and other Malay friends, many of whom were from peninsular Malaya. They lent me fresh clothing and gave me bedding. The next day, when the curfew was lifted briefly, I accepted the offer of a lift home to Serangoon Gardens from an Indian boy who also lived there.

This display of racial harmony was repeated in the September 1964 race riots. This time, I was in the Students' Union bus together with a mixed-race group of undergraduates. A couple of Indian boys had commandeered the bus to send us home before the start of the curfew.

In this political turmoil between Singapore and Kuala Lumpur, an unusual event occurred in the university. The Kuala Lumpur government had all along been anti-left because of its experience of the Malayan Communist Party-inspired Emergency. So it was strange that in the months before August 1965, the government invited Socialist Club members on an all-expenses-paid trip to Kuala Lumpur as a 'making friends gesture'. While the busload of students were in Kuala Lumpur on the morning of 9 August 1965, Prime Minister Lee Kuan Yew went on television and radio to announce the separation from Malaysia.

Until 9 August 1965, the concept of a Singaporean did not exist. People with even the scantiest of knowledge about Singapore's economic dependence on the entrepôt trade felt only trepidation about leaving Malaysia. We had always thought of ourselves as Malayans and this attitude prevailed among the English-educated of all races. Many of us had relatives up north. Many of us were born there and came to Singapore because we saw economic and educational opportunities that did not exist in the small Malayan towns where we were born. Several of the PAP's leaders – Dr Goh Keng Swee and Dr Toh Chin Chye for example – were Malayan-born.

Up until August 1965, there was free movement of people between Singapore and Malaya. No one carried a passport and we shared a common cur-

The three-week boycott protesting a curriculum review in Nanyang University ended when police helped willing students to return to class, November 1965.

rency. Years later, I would read about the obstacles that Dr Goh faced in trying to realise his vision to transform the Singapore economy during the Malaysia years. In 1965, surviving without the Malayan hinterland and its primary commodities economy had seemed impossible.

Happily, 55 years down the road, however traumatic the events were that led to the birth of our country, there is no Singaporean today who does not think that independence was the best thing to happen.

In 1959, soon after the first general elections, Dr Toh Chin Chye announced the government's plan to introduce a coat of arms, flag and anthem although, at that time, the British had no plans to grant Singapore independence. Dr Toh, who was the prime mover behind these emblems, explained years later that they were designed to bring together the different races as a Singapore nation. He was prescient.

As these symbols of nationhood were introduced during National Solidarity Week in 1959, it meant that Singapore had already in place a state crest, flag and national anthem when we became an independent country in 1965.

BUKIT TIMAH, SINGAPORE
Lee Tzu Pheng

This highway I know,
the only way into the city
where the muddy canal goes.
These are the sides of coarse grasses
where the schoolboys stumble in early morning
wet-staining their white shoes.

This is the way the city is fed,
men, machines,
flushed out of their short dreams
and suburban holes
to churn down this waiting gullet.
They flow endlessly this way
from dawn, before sky opens,
to the narrow glare of noon
and evening's slow closing.

NOTE: *The poet's family moved to
Bukit Timah from Katong in 1955 and
lived there till well beyond the 1960s.*

Under the steaming morning,
ambition flashes by in a new car;
the reluctant salesman faced
with another day of selling his pride
hunches over the lambretta, swerving
from old farmer with fruit-heavy basket.
The women back from market
remark that this monsoon will be bad
for the price of vegetables;
their loitering children, too small for school,
learn the value of five cents, ten cents,
from hunger and these market days.

All morning the tired buses whine
their monotonous route, drag
from stop to stop,
disgorge schoolchildren, pale-faced clerks,
long-suffering civil servants,
pretty office girls, to feed
the megalopolitan appetite.

This highway I know,
the only way out of the city:
the same highway under the moon,
the same people under the sea-green
of lamps newly turned on at evening.

One day there will be tall buildings
here, where the green trees reach
for the narrow canal.
The holes where the restless sleepers are
will be neat, boxed-up in ten-stories.
Life will be orderly, comfortable,
exciting, occasionally, at the new nightclubs.

I wonder what that old farmer would say,
if he lived to come this way.

LEFT: Misty morning, Mount Faber, 1959. Opened on 17 January 1965, Mount Faber Park was designed atop the 106-m hill. It was named in 1845 after Captain Charles Edward Faber of the Madras Engineers who built a narrow, winding road to the summit for a signal station and flagstaff. Before that, the second highest hill in Singapore was named Telok Blangah Hill.

TOP: Nine holes before the work day, c 1962. In 1958, the City Council mistakenly sent a demand to the Royal Island Club to open its grounds to the public by June 1959. Self-government in May 1959 intervened and the club kept the land for members' use only.

OVERLEAF: Tai chi, 1963. The Padang has seen movements of all kinds. On 3 June 1959, the People's Action Party-led first Legislative Assembly of Singapore held a victory rally on the lawn fronting City Hall.

FACING: The quiet South Boat Quay early in the morning, 1960.

ABOVE: Esplanade Food Centre, 1962. The 21 stalls arrayed in a crescent opened on 15 November 1952, making it possibly Singapore's first modern hawker centre.

LEFT: Kallang Basin, c 1962, where ship-builders and charcoal traders centered in the 1950s and 60s.

PREVIOUS: Prawn catcher and clam diggers, 1950s. Prawning in the shallows and scraping sand for *siput remis* were happy, fruitful activities.

LEFT: People of the Sea, Bedok, 1962. Remnant populations of the *orang laut* lived in Kampong Siglap, Kampong Bedok and other villages of the east coast.

ABOVE: On a *kelong*, 1962. Fishing platforms and stakes of bakau wood lined the coast from Siglap to Tanah Merah.

LEFT: Punggol estuary, 1962. Pig and poultry farms surrounded a river mouth that hid crocodiles.

RIGHT & BELOW: Farms, 1960s. Self-sufficiency was the aim of food production in the post-war period. On 25 June 1959, the agriculture, co-operatives, fisheries, rural development and veterinary divisions under the Ministry of National Development became the Primary Production Department. It managed some 15,000 hectres of farmland dotted around Singapore.

FACING: Pig farm, Kampong Ang Mo Kio, 1962. Pig farms kept swine by the hundreds to the thousands while smallholders would rear a few to be fattened and served or sold. The feed was swill collected by the household and from neighbours.

LEFT: Chickens being vaccinated, 1960s. Vaccination and breeding programmes for pigs and poultry were conducted by the Primary Production Department.

BELOW: Transporting pigs, 1960. Pigs, caged in rattan baskets, were brought to the slaughterhouse in trucks or even by bicycle.

LEFT: Chinese kampong folk, 1960s. Village settlements of mainly Chinese focussed on farming – both vegetables and fish or prawns, plantation agriculture and serving British military communities. Nee Soon, Upper Sernagoon, Bishan, Bukit Merah, Bukit Panjang, Jurong, and Tampines were but a few of the many Chinese kampong areas.

ABOVE: Rediffusion set in a kampong home, 1960s. A cable-transmitted radio station, Rediffusion became the staple form of entertainment for some 50,000 subscribers in the 1960s. Popular presenters such as Lee Dai Soh who told stories in Cantonese attracted over 100,000 listeners.

PREVIOUS, LEFT & RIGHT: Malay kampongs were ranged along the coast – Woodlands, Bedok, Pasir Ris, Geylang – and on the southern islands. Fishing and coconut planting were the main activities.

BELOW: Bendemeer Road, 1963. Toa Payoh, Kampong Bahru, Punggol and Sembawang were some of the other areas where different races lived together in kampongs. Pasir Ris was notable for its Indian villagers rearing cattle among Chinese smallholders.

PREVIOUS: A village shop in Eunos, 1960s. *Sarikat* means 'company, people working together or united for business purposes', thus a cooperative.

TOP LEFT: Installing overhead electricity lines, 1963. Light at the flick of a switch in the 1960s, courtesy of the Rural and Urban Services Advisory Council, was introduced to selected kampong areas based on population density and ease of installation.

ABOVE: Heading to the market at Changi Village, 1960s. The village was no kampong, but a hive of shops serving the servicemen and their families stationed in RAF Changi.

LEFT: Paving a village path, 1964. Jalan Serigading, expunged from Kampong Ubi, was named after *Nyctanthes abortristis*, the Night-flowering Jasmine.

ABOVE: Water distribution by tanker, 1959.

TOP RIGHT: Standpipe construction, Jurong, 1959.

BOTTOM RIGHT: Running tap water, Geylang Serai, 1960.

Domestic water consumption in 1960 was 40.79 million cubic metres per annum (compared to 495.5 million cubic metres in 2018). With no aquifers and significant rivers and lakes, rainfall was the chief water source for Singapore.

In 1959, the City Council commissioned a $2 million groundwater system in Bedok which, disappointingly, yielded less than 10 percent of the expected 10 million gallons per day.

Singapore was therefore heavily reliant on water from Johore, resulting in the City Council signing water agreements with the Malayan authorities in October 1961 and September 1962.

In 1963, during a period of prolonged dry weather, the Council imposed 10 months of water rationing.

The Rural and Urban Services Advisory Council launched a water supply scheme in the 1960s, but some villages would not get piped water until a decade later.

BELOW: Mobile nursing team, 1960s. The Singapore Trained Nurses' Association gained associate membership of the International Council of Nurses in 1959, the year when the *Handbook on Nursing Procedures* was published in Sinagpore. Mobile dispensaries, including floating ones, travelled to kampongs on the mainland and on islands to provide inoculations and basic health care.

BOTTOM RIGHT: Post-natal care, 1962. Infant mortality was 34.9 deaths per thousand live-births in 1960. Home births, assisted by *bidan*s or midwives, were the norm, beds in maternity hospitals being in short supply. Thus, trained nurses from government-run Maternal and Child Health Centres made house calls to provide before- and after-birth care.

RIGHT: Portrait of siblings, 1963. The total births per woman in 1960 was 5.76 (compared with 1.14 in 2018). In the 1960s, the government funded the Family Planning Association of Singapore, a volunteer group which operated numerous sexual health clinics offering contraception and marital advice.

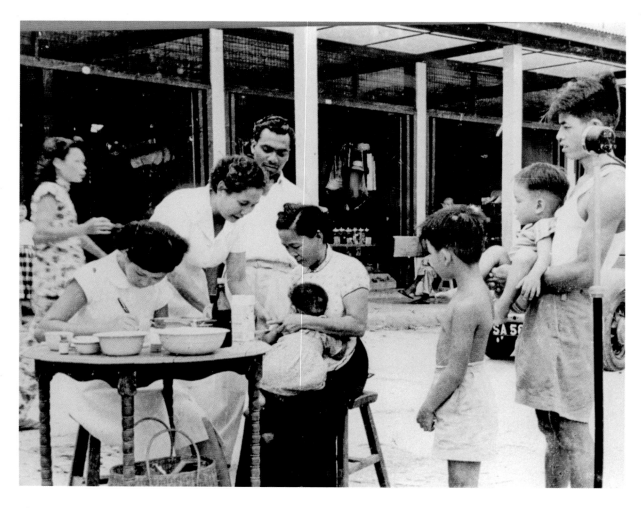

PREVIOUS: Silat Integrated School, c1960. Chinese school enrolment was 45.9 percent of all students in 1959. The integration scheme, from 1960, which put students from two or more language streams together fostered better race relations.

ABOVE: Mixed gender school, 1959. In the mid-1950s, 50 percent more boys than girls were enrolled in primary school. By 1965, universal primary education was achieved.

BOTTOM LEFT: Students of Tampines Primary School, 1964. With independence, the focus was for a 'Singaporean Singapore' based on racial equality and a Singaporean identity.

BELOW: School friends, 1960. Lining up children according to height was popular for group photos of children in the 1950s and 60s. Here, boys from Lee Teck Public School in Ulu Sembawang take the ladder pose literally.

RIGHT: Three Little Pigs, 1960s. English-medium schools, decidedly Anglophile in outlook, taught students English nursery rhymes and fairy tales.

ABOVE: Seletar Primary School, 1959. The school, which catered to the children of RAF servicemen, was in the airbase which had oh-so-English road names: Brompton, Maida Vale, Piccadilly, and so on.

LEFT: RAF Seletar, Sergeants' Mess, 1960s. The address: 1 Park Lane.

TOP RIGHT: 'Sew Sew woman' and shoeshine man, RAF Seletar, 1950s. Sew Sew women were so called because they provided sewing and mending services for RAF servicemen. Likewise, Indian men polished the shoes and boots of the soldiers.

RIGHT: Swimmers at RAF Seletar, pre-1963. The original swimming pool at Seletar was a large water tank. Over time, the pool was upgraded, the most significant of which was completed in 1963.

ABOVE: Servicing a Flying Boat, 1950s. The RAF's Short S.25 Sunderland petrol bombers remained in use in the Far East post-war. The last two Sunderlands of Seletar alighted after their final flight on 15 May 1959, the year when the RAF withdrew the aircraft from military service.

RIGHT: The city from 5,000 feet up, 10 November 1962. This photograph by the RAF shows highrises on the waterfront, including Bank of China building (1953), Asia Insurance Building (1955) and the 15-storey Shell House (1960).

OVERLEAF: Rochor Circus, 1963. This busy traffic hub connected Rochor Canal Road, Rochor Road, Jalan Besar, Sungei Road and Bencoolen Street.

LEFT & ABOVE: *Majie*, 1960. Amahs or black and white servants were Cantonese women, former silk production workers from Shunde in the Pearl River delta, who immigrated to Singapore and other British colonies to work as domestic helpers.

They were always addressed by their given names followed by *jie*, meaning elder sister. Thus Lan *jie*, Kum *jie*, Heong *jie*.

The *majie* belonged to a sworn, celibate sisterhood who wore their hair either in a long plait or, ironically, in a tight bun behind the head that traditionally identified married women in China. Their uniform was the samfoo, dark loose trousers over light tops, hence the reference to black and white.

Some worked 'one leg kick', a Cantonese phrase which describes the multitude of tasks that the *majie* must perform in her employer's household:

cooking, childcare and housekeeping. Others who worked for affluent families who employed a large staff performed just one domestic role.

On weekends, these live-in maids returned to the *kongsi fong*, their shared amah association accommodations in Chinatown, to spend time with their community.

LEFT: Sago Street, 1961. Cellophane and silk lanterns festooned the streets of Dai Por, the Cantonese area of Chinatown south of the Singapore River, during the Mid-Autumn Festival.

Traditional foods of the season were pomelo, *lengkok* (water caltrop), and, of course, mooncakes filled with lotus paste – some with salted egg yolks – or mixed nuts bound by treacle.

BELOW: Bucket system, c 1959. Toilets required users to squat over holes under which were placed metal collection buckets.

The euphemism 'nightsoil' derives from the practice of scooping earth over the waste to minimise the stench.

Small doors at the back of shophouses allowed the bucket to be extracted and carried away on either side of a pole over the shoulder or in trucks of many compartments.

Remarkably, the bucket system only came to an end in 1987.

TOP LEFT: Boats by the quay, 1960s. At low tide all is quiet, but the jam of barges shows that business is brisk for the *towkay* of South Boat Quay.

The quay defined the Belly of the Carp, the shape of the river basin considered auspicious by the businesses that occupied the 108 shophouses that lined the curve.

LEFT & ABOVE: Lightermen, c 1960. Wiry, sun-baked and muscular, coolies shouldered cargo on springy gangplanks from boats into the quayside warehouses. Hefting sacks of 50-100 kilos, they were the backbone of the river trade.

Family businesses employed their own labourers. They lived with the company clerks and cook above the offices and were provided with simple meals.

OVERLEAF: Bumboats, 1962. The flat-bottomed bumboats, also known as *twakow,* carried goods from ships anchored off-shore to the river bank.

With painted eyes to show the way and old tyres as bumpers, they were part and parcel of the Singapore riverscape until their decline began with the introduction of mechanisation and container shipping.

The last cargo-carrying bumboat finally went, chugging out to its new moorage in Pasir Panjang in September 1983.

ABOVE: Tai Tong Restaurant, 1962.

LEFT: Porridge for breakfast, 1963.

TOP RIGHT: A hearty street-side hawker meal.

RIGHT: Sharing noodles, 1962.

OVERLEAF: Eating at Waterloo Street, 1962.

Food was home-cooked, or from restaurants and street-side stalls. Dishes of all kinds, eaten while seated on stools at appropriately low tables, could be bought from hawkers parked at their usual spots. Otherwise, you listened for the calls or the tick-tock of bamboo clappers announcing the approach of roaming vendors who carried their portable kitchens with them.

LEFT: A Sikh watchman and his wife, 1964. Makhan Singh Gill records his first day of work with a snapshot in his Cecil Street home. Watchmen, or *jaga* – some who were former policemen – guarded banks, shops and godowns.

BELOW: Milkman, c 1959. Milk was delivered fresh from the source, with the milking of cows done right at the doorstep. Otherwise, milk in cans came from farms via bicycles.

Indians had provided this service since the 1840s. Hence, Kerbau (buffalo) Road in Little India and Palkadei Saddaku – Milk Shop Street – now Cecil Street.

RIGHT: Serangoon Road snapshot, 1962. Indians formed 9 percent of Singapore's population c 1959.

Around this time, the iconic businesses of Little India were being founded: Lian Seng for household goods, Haniffa Textiles, Jothi flower shop, and Mustafa which started as a food stall.

The successful South Indian merchant P. Govindasamy Pillai was then on the brink of retirement and handing over his chain of PGP provision and textile shops to his children.

ABOVE: Children in Hindu temple grounds, 1963. In 1959, 70 percent of the Indian population was Hindu and 20 percent Muslim. By profession, they were merchants, civil servants and soldiers or practised traditional trades. Tamils, Malayalees and Punjabis made up the majority of the Indian sub-groups.

LEFT: Chatting at a wedding, Sri Mariamman Temple, 1963.

TOP RIGHT: A prayer for blessing during a wedding ceremony, Sri Mariamman Temple, 1964. Statistics for the 1960s show that arranged marriages were the norm among Indians, with half the brides being teenagers.

RIGHT: Receiving *kalanji*, a traditional honour, Sri Mariamman Temple, 1960.

PREVIOUS & LEFT:
Kuan Im Thong Hood
Cho Temple, Waterloo
Street, 1962.

RIGHT: Women at a
temple door, 1965.

Leon Comber writes
in *Chinese Temples in
Singapore*, published 1958,
that Kuan Im Thong
Hood Cho Temple,
'hemmed in by stalls,
fortune-teller booths, and
shops selling religious
articles, is extremely
popular with Chinese
women.'
   Buddhist temples,
associations and societies,
supported by prominent
Buddhists, had petitioned
Governor Franklin
Gimson in 1949 to
make Vesak Day a public
holiday. However, it
came to pass only in 1955
under Chief Minister
David Marshall.

BELOW: Mee Chong Goldsmith, 1965. Gold, valued by all races, was bought for investment and as gifts for rites of passage. Goldsmithing became a traditional trade, with shops in North and South Bridge roads, and craftsmen in Little India. Jewellery purchased in Chinatown were often packaged and taken away in pink, plastic boxes.

RIGHT: Joo Chiat, 1962. This vibrant, easy-going neighbourhood of pastel-coloured shophouses, kampongs and cinemas was famous for iconic food. The Malay, Chinese, Eurasian and Peranakan communities who lived in this area could get seafood fresh from the beach, canned goods from Tay Buan Guan supermarket, cream cakes from Red House Bakery and spicy noodles from Jangok Katong Laksa.

BOTTOM RIGHT: Peddler, 1960. Hawkers offered more than food. There were itinerant haberdasheries, hardware stores and vendors of household goods and cleaning equipment. Each brought their products right to the doorsteps of housewives.

OVERLEAF: Street markets, 1960s. Vendors sold more than edibles; they offered everything under the sun, from crockery to underwear. But this was not the only way to shop. There were five purpose-built covered markets selling foodstuff in Rochor, Orchard Road, Ellenborough Street, Clyde Terrace and Telok Ayer.

PREVIOUS: Traffic in Joo Chiat, 1963. Manual traffic direction belied police power. From the mid-1950s, the Police Radio Division's 24-hour operation room had 13 networks and a fleet of 60 patrol cars.

RIGHT: Harbour roads, 1963. Ships of all kinds hide the horizon. By 1965, Singapore was the fifth largest port in the world.

BELOW: View from Clifford Pier, 1962. The 18-storey, 73.5-metre, $8-million Art Deco Asia Insurance Building was completed in 1955. Designed by architect Ng Keng Siang, it received high praise from the Singapore Municipal Commissioners who recognised that the building 'would, by its majesty, beautify Singapore's waterfront, gaining indirect benefit from its advertisement.'

FACING: Trishaws at Collyer Quay, 1962. Depending on the hours spent cycling and the numbers of passengers, trishaw riders earned between $3 and $20 daily.

LEFT: Young working adults, Fullerton Square, 1963. Behind the youthful, modern façade were many challenges: a small domestic market with low per capita income, no natural resources, over-dependence on entrepôt trade, reliance on the British military for employment, a small industrial base, low literacy, and high unemployment.

RIGHT: Raffles Place from the Shriro (China) office, c 1962. Singapore relied on imported goods, and Shriro's supplies included pharmaceuticals, watches, photographic equipment and cosmetics.

BELOW: Change Alley, 1959. This 100-metre lane linked Collyer Quay and Raffles Place. Ground-floor shops sold a mind-boggling array of goods and moneychangers swopped cash for tourists to buy them. Here, you had to bargain and watch out for pickpockets.

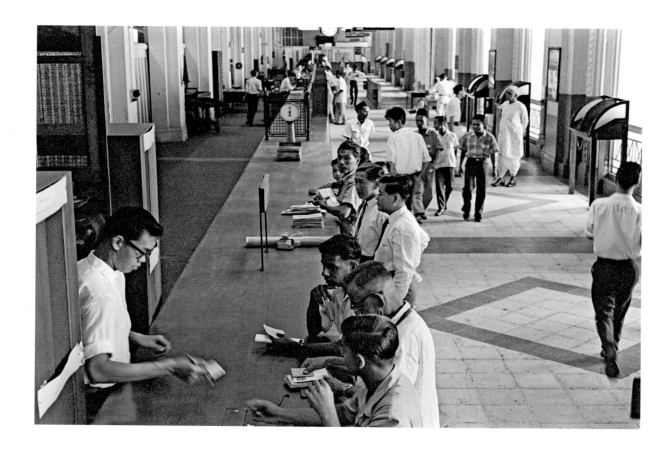

PREVIOUS: Thai Airways and Scandinavian Airlines System office, Raffles Place, 1962. The domestic carrier was Malayan Airlines, 'domestic' being the operative word as its routes covered just Singapore, Kuala Lumpur, Ipoh and Penang till 1960. Afterwhich, new routes were added: Singapore to Hong Kong, and Kuala Lumpur to Bangkok via Penang.

ABOVE & TOP RIGHT: General Post Office, 1965. In 1960, 32 post offices run by the Singapore Postal Department served rural and urban populations. Post boxes were red pillars. Mail was sorted by hand. Ironically, the stamp commemorating self-government in 1959 kept the portrait of the British queen.

RIGHT: Office workers, 1963. In 1965, business services formed 23.7 percent of the economy, wholesale and retail trade 20 percent and manufacturing 14.2 percent. The GDP per capita was $1,580. The labour force numbered 701,700, of which women formed only about 20 percent.

LEFT: Stock exchange trading hall, 1962. Everything was manual with prices written on blackboards. In 1965, 207 brokers and dealers traded shares of 204 listed companies worth 89 million units.

BOTTOM LEFT: Currency exchange, 1962. That year, a Singapore dollar fetched USD 0.33, AUD 0.29, RMB 0.8, and GBP 0.12.

RIGHT: Beggar along Battery Road, 1963. This was a time when a bowl of noodles cost twenty cents and a slice of cake five cents. At the other extreme, a freehold Holland Road terrace house cost $28,000. In 1960, the median monthly wage for trained employees was $120.

OVERLEAF: Singapore River mouth, 1960s. The river was more than a river of commerce. Children swam in it, people lived in boats on it and in shophouses along its banks. The Singapore River was a community.

114

LEFT: Big Walk, 1964. The *Singapore Free Press*-sponsored inaugural walk in 1960 drew 3,500 racers. The route covered 14.5 miles from Woodlands to Farrer Park with some 120,000 spectators cheering on the competitors. These foot races were fixtures on the sporting calendar beyond the 1960s.

BOTTOM LEFT & BELOW: School sports day, 1960s. Popular events included vaulting over hurdles, egg-and-spoon challenges, sack races and beanbag relays. Victors won miniature metal trophies mounted on bakelite bases.

OVERLEAF: Free milk, 1950s. From post-World War II until the 1960s, milk was provided free to needy children. Supplied by UNICEF, skimmed milk and a wheat-soya blended drink were distributed by the Social Welfare Department to welfare institutions and schools. In the last quarter of 1961, the amount given was 19,753 lbs (8,960 kg).

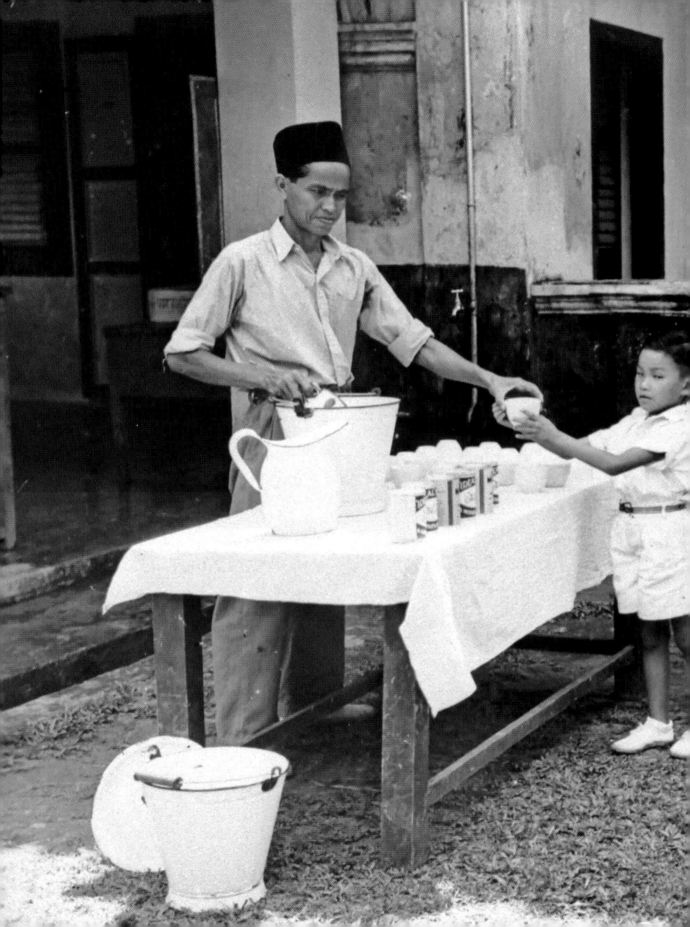

ABOVE & RIGHT:
Public crèches, 1964.
In the mid-1960s, the
Department of Social
Welfare ran 10 crèches
catering to low-income
families. With the rise
of household incomes,
the income ceiling for
enrolment was raised
from $300 to $400 per
month in 1964.

LEFT: Children's home,
1963. The policy of the
Children's Department
of the Department of
Social Welfare was to
employ staff based on
personality, not academic
qualifications. The
inclusion of in-service
training made this
practice possible.

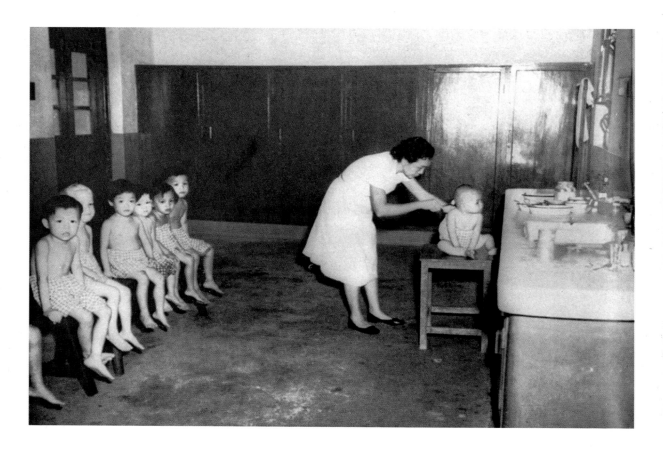

ABOVE: Medical checkup, 1960s. Infant mortality rate in 1959 was 36 per 1,000 live births. Diseases of early infancy caused 9 percent of all deaths. From 1961 to 1964, 4.1 percent of the government budget was spent on building hospitals and maternity homes, expand existing ones and starting 17 outpatient clinics.

In 1961, all government medical services were put under the Public Health Division responsible for preventive health services, student, maternal and child health, health education and the regulation of markets and hawkers.

TOP RIGHT: St Andrew's Mission Hospital, 1962. In the 1950s, one in every 50 new children seen at the hospital had tuberculosis, most too late for treatment. The government mandated compulsory vaccination. By reaching 85 percent of infants each year through a vaccination programme, common infectious illnesses in children were eliminated.

RIGHT: Indian father and son, 1962. Indians formed 8 percent of the population in 1960 while Chinese comprised 76 percent, Malay 14 percent and other races 2 percent. Of a total population of 1,633,717, those under the age of five numbered 301,996 or 8.9 percent.

OVERLEAF: Head-shaving ritual, 1962. The Hindu ritual of *mundan* or the first hair cut, done in the first or third year of a child's life, is a rite of purification.

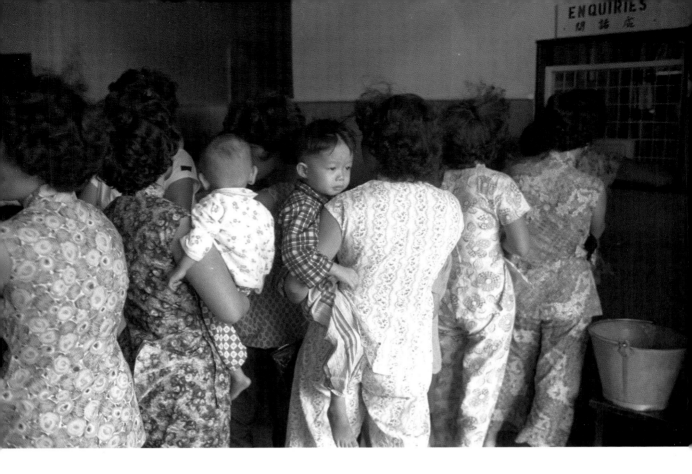

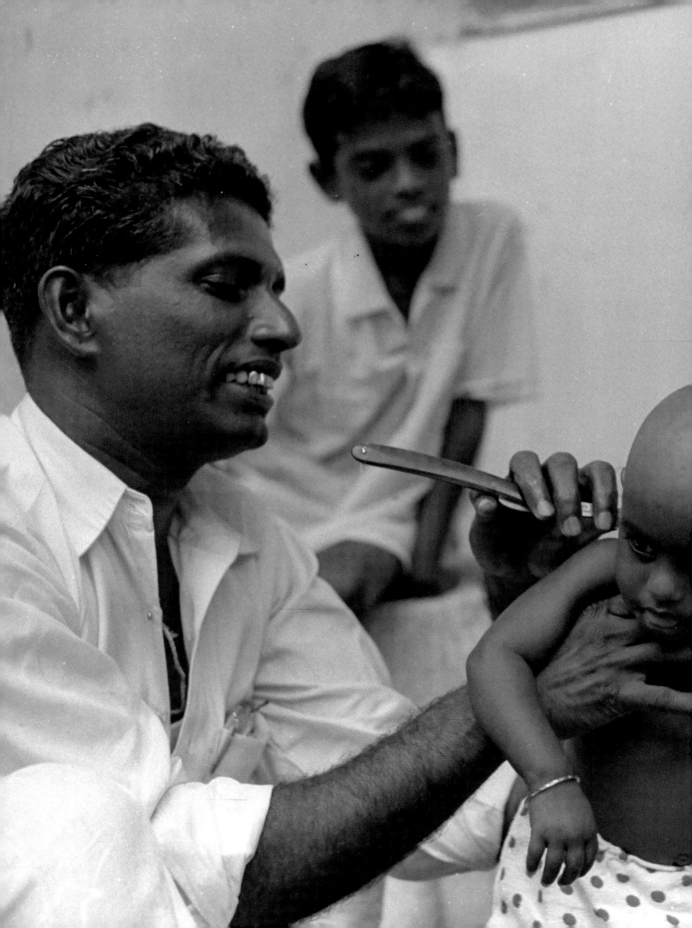

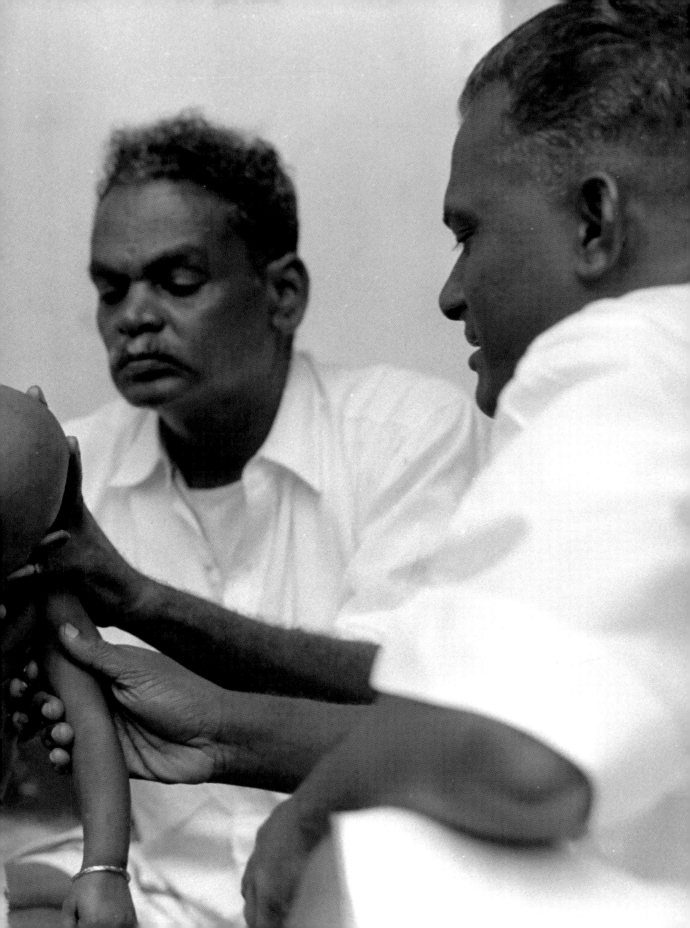

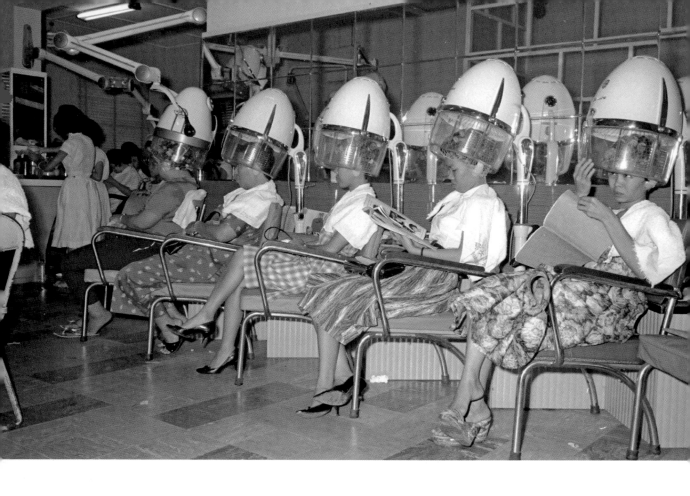

ABOVE: Getting a permanent wave, 1960. Good salons advertised 'London trained' hairdressers. Locally trained hairdressers charged $4–5 for a perm, $2 for cut-and-wash, while colouring cost some $25 per treatment.

LEFT: Young couple, 1962. People married young in the early 1960s, 23 being the average age for women, and 27 for men.

ABOVE & LEFT: Housewives, 1960s. In the late 1950s, the literacy rate among females was 30 percent. As most women, except the daughters of the rich, were left uneducated, expected to be housewives, and not encouraged to find work or make a career, they were financially dependent on men.

Ironically, the gender-blind education policy of the early 1960s did not give special attention to females. The assumption was that the uneven playing field faced by women and girls would level up as education was made available to both boys and girls.

OVERLEAF: Mass wedding, 1960. Chinese community groups organised such weddings up to the early 1960s. A fee of $30 to $40 bought you the venue, decorations, music, simple refreshments and a wedding certificate signed by a senior member of the organising association or a well-known community figure.

Mass weddings, which celebrated common law marriages, declined rapidly upon the passing of the Women's Charter in 1961 which mandated the registration of marriages with the Registry of Marriages and gave legal rights in marriage to women.

ABOVE: Tourist Promotion Board staff members, 1964.

LEFT: Immigration counter, 1965.

Singapore: The Lion City, the 1957 tourism documentary produced by the Malayan Film Unit advertised 'such variety, such contrast, and all in so small a space' and highlighted Raffles Hotel, the 'world famous' Change Alley, the Great World, Happy World,

New World amusement parks, Paya Lebar Airport, and the city's cleanliness.

The Singapore Tourist Promotion Board and its Merlion emblem both came about in 1964, and initial promotions focused on attracting visitors from the United States, Australia and Japan.

ABOVE: Second-class carriage on the train going up country, 1963. First-class carriages in the early 1960s were carpeted and furnished with arm chairs and coffee tables among which waiters moved, offering food and drink, including beer.

RIGHT: Malay, Chinese, Western and Indian exotic beauties of 1960s Singapore.

OVERLEAF: Paya Lebar Airport, 1962. Seven years after the airport's opening, its runway was extended in 1962 for the use of large jets. At 9,000 feet (2,750 metres), it was one of the longest runways in Asia at the time.

In the final phase of the airport's development, a new passenger terminal was opened in 1964.

LEFT: Raffles Hotel, 1962. This was the hotel Somerset Maugham saw on his last visit in 1960. His first stay was in 1921 when he sat in the Palm Court, correcting proofs of one of his books.

BELOW: Haw Par Villa, 1960s. Also known as Tiger Balm Gardens, this park – based on Chinese mythology and folklore – was on the itinerary of many tourists and featured on technicolour postcards. Its dioramas of the Ten Courts of Hell were vividly used by Chinese parents to bring home the consequences of not being filial.

RIGHT: A pierced *kavadi* carrier, 1962. Thaipusam is a Hindu festival of thanksgiving and fulfillment of vows promised to Lord Murugan. It was a public holiday through the early 1960s when devotees as young as the age of 13 were allowed to be pierced.

ALL: *Kopitiam*, 1965. The Hainanese-run coffee shops and the equivalent Malay *kedai kopi* and Indian *sarabat* stalls were where people of every race and background met for a hot drink (*o*, *siew dai* or *kosong*) and a quick snack while engaging in coffee-shop talk.

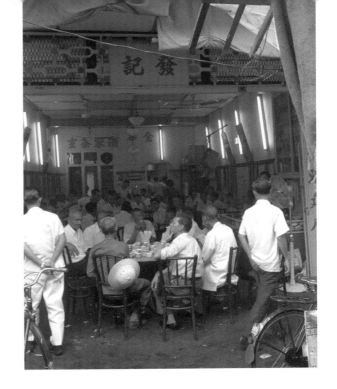

LEFT: Making rattan chairs, 1959. This workshop was a social enterprise in Children's Social Centres run by the Department of Social Welfare.

Going beyond a feeding programme, it gave older children vocational training: carpentry and rattan weaving for boys and sewing and knitting for girls.

BELOW: Shoe factory, 1960s. For uneducated women, jobs were few, if any. Beyond being a washerwoman, some aspired to be hospital attendants.

Factory jobs were limited to those available in old-school industries such as soft-drink bottling and shoe-making until the government invited foreign firms to start manufacturing plants as part of its strategy to move the economy from import substitution to export-oriented manufacturing.

FACING: Foundation stone laying ceremony at the National Steel Mills, Jurong Industrial Estate, 1962. The first economic development blueprint after self-government in 1959 focused on expanding manufacturing which, in 1960, represented just 11.4 percent of the GDP.

The Winsemius Report of 1961, the result of the United Nations Industrial Survey Mission led by Albert Winsemius, recommended ship repairing, shipbuilding and metal engineering as industries that could be developed in the long term.

LEFT: Opening of the Swan brand socks factory, Jurong Industrial Estate, 1964.

BELOW: A Japanese economic delegation visiting Jurong Industrial Estate, 1962. In 1961, Finance Minister, Dr Goh Keng Swee, kicked off the transformation of Jurong from a swampy and hilly backwoods into an industrial estate filled with factories started by foreign firms. To keep the momentum going, foreign economic delegations were invited to tour the site and every factory opening was celebrated.

TOP AND BOTTOM LEFT: Jurong Wharf under construction, 1963. Jurong's natural deep-water harbour was the decisive factor for Jurong being chosen as Singapore's first industrial estate. Work on the port to serve the industries there began in January 1961 and was completed in November 1965. The first ship to dock, the SS *President Van Buren*, arrived in January 1966.

ABOVE: Singapore Harbour, 1960s. The 1957 Report of the Commission of Inquiry into the Port of Singapore, which recommended the establishment of a single authority to manage the whole port, was accepted by the government in 1963. Thus, on 1 April 1964, the functions of the Singapore Harbour Board and Master Attendant came under the Port of Singapore Authority.

PREVIOUS: Hawker stall, Prince Philip Avenue, 1963.

LEFT: Hawkers in Queenstown Market, 1963.

Hawking gave work to the unemployed, and provided affordable food. But concerns about hygiene led to the licensing of hawkers in the early 1950s and illegal hawkers literally had their means of livelihood destroyed. This continued through the 1960s, until the first dedicated hawker centre was built in Jurong in 1972.

ABOVE: Family portrait, St Michael's Estate, 1964. Although women in Singapore began entering the workforce in the 1950s and 60s, their primary roles were still housekeeping and caring for their children.

This double duty meant that women chose shift work in factories or other jobs which gave them enough time to complete their housework when they returned home.

RIGHT & BELOW:
Lunchtime in Chinatown,
1960s. A herbal tea shop
and a meal shared by the
roadside.

FACING: Office workers
having lunch, 1960s. For
white-collar workers
from Raffles Place, one
popular option for lunch
was the row of hawkers
wedged between Bank of
China and the Singapore
River.

LEFT: Five-foot-way library, Chinatown, 1962. The comics were of Chinese tales and folklore – *Romance of the Three Kingdoms*, *The Water Margin* – while the magazines featured stars of Singapore-owned Shaw and Cathay studios.

RIGHT & BELOW: National Library, Stamford Road, 1962. The red-brick, fair-faced building, designed by the Public Works Department, was opened in 1960. Its collections in English, Chinese, Malay and Tamil for adults and children, a microfilm unit, and a lecture hall, covered a floor area of 10,242 square metres.

OVERLEAF: National Museum, 1964. The Raffles Museum was renamed National Museum in 1960 but retained its ethnography and natural history character showing collections from the colonial era.

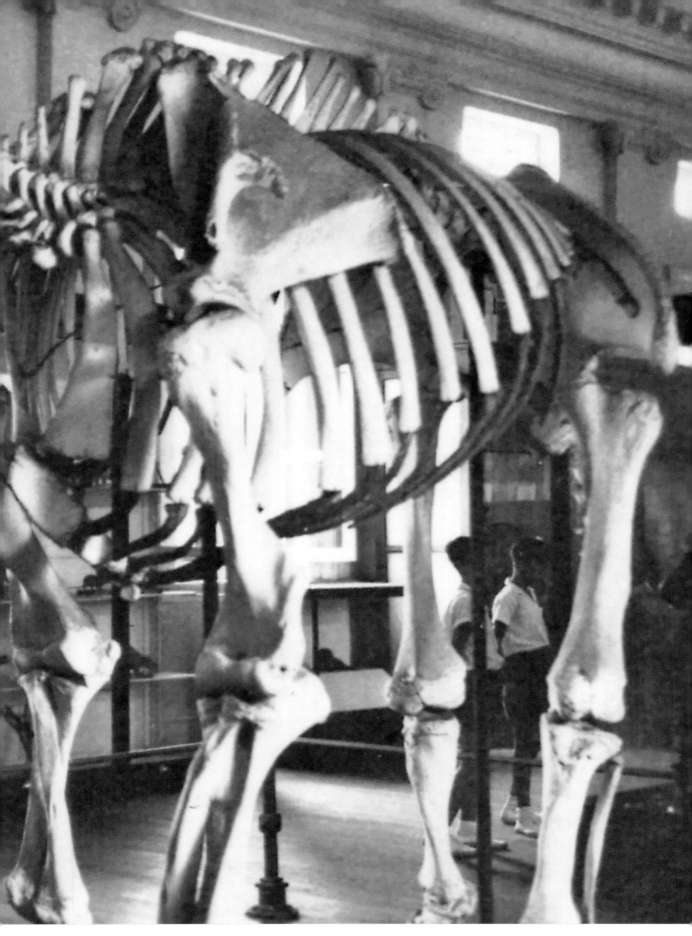

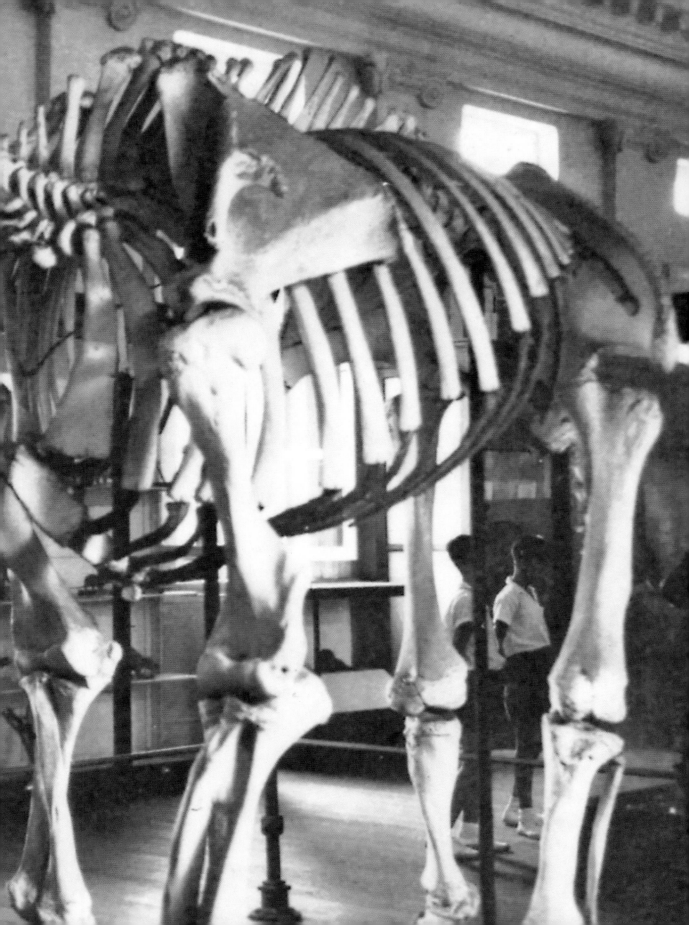

ABOVE: Monkeys at the Botanic Gardens, 1960s. In 1961, some 300 long-tailed macaques, described as 'the worst pest' in the press, badly damaged plants in the Gardens.

Efforts to shoot them were unsuccessful as a single shot would scatter the monkeys to the tree tops. The rise in the number of monekys may well have been caused by visitors feeding the animals.

TOP RIGHT: Bandstand, Botanic Gardens, 1960s. The iconic gazebo stood as it did when it was built in 1930 as there had been only minor changes to the garden landscape from then to the 1960s.

After 1965, the Botanic Gardens moved from botanical research to providing horticultural support for Singapore's Garden City vision.

RIGHT: Hawkers outside the Botanic Gardens, 1965. With the registration of hawkers mooted in 1959, the stalls at the garden gates soon became illegal. Hawker food became available again at the Botanic Gardens when the Taman Serasi Food Centre was opened in 1974.

OVERLEAF: Singapore Ice-Cream Sellers Cooperative Society, 1962. Incorporated in 1960 by 96 ice-cream hawkers, the cooperative's factory in Sims Avenue produced two tons of ice-cream per day.

ABOVE: Hawker selling aiyu jelly, Selegie Road, 1963. With the registration of hawkers in the 1960s, a common appeal by the unempolyed in meet-the-people sessions was for help to obtain a hawker licence.

LEFT: *Muruku* man, c 1960. Buying Indian spiced snacks outside a house in Chancery Lane.

FACING: Party at F&N Hall, 1962. Volunteer organisations such as the Hans Andersen Club and corporations like Fraser & Neave hosted parties regularly for children from low-income households.

Red Lion, a drink in orange or pineapple flavours, was launched in 1955 and remained popular through the 1960s.

OVERLEAF: Children at play, 1962. *Captek*, *kuti-kuti*, five stones, hopscotch, *gasing* and even *tikam-tikam* – games played by children of every race.

ABOVE: Koran lesson, Katong, 1962. In 1959, there were 12 *madrasah* (Muslim schools) in Singapore, increasing to 28 by 1962.

LEFT: Studying at home. The Primary School Leaving Examination, introduced in 1960, was intended to integrate schools of different language streams through a common syllabus.

RIGHT: Nanyang University library, 1960. The private Chinese-language university produced 437 graduates in 1959 with enrolment increasing to 2,324 in 1963.

BELOW: Schoolgirls at Queen Street, 1962. The literacy rate of females in Singapore was 34 percent in 1957. Not surprising then that in 1960, females accounted for 23 percent of university enrolment in Singapore.

LEFT & ABOVE: Junction of Orchard, Scotts and Paterson roads, 1960s. In 1958, the air-conditioned Fitzpatrick's Supermarket and C K Tang department store opened in Orchard Road. A year later, the up-market Lido cinema and the Rosee d'Or Room restaurant and nightclub started business in Shaw House.

RIGHT: Nepali traders, 1960. Among the offerings – semi-precious stones of garnet, beryl, and tourmaline.

ABOVE: Raffles Place, 1959. Robinsons and John Little were the anchor shops of this commercial centre. On 27 November 1965, an underground carpark with spaces for 250 cars and a roof garden opened in the middle of the square.

LEFT: Product and Design Display Centre in John Little, 1965.

RIGHT: A shop in the Arcade, 1962. Linking Collyer Quay to Raffles Place and lined with shops, the Arcade was perhaps Singapore's first shopping mall.

LEFT: High fashion from High Street, 1965. This was the shopping street where Metro started as Metrotex, and Sindhi and Sikh shopkeepers offered Swiss voile and other luxurious fabrics.

Also famous here was TMA, a music shop run by Tan Peck Soo, the godfather of 1960s Singapore pop who helped up-and-coming musicians purchase high-quality instruments through painless loans.

ABOVE: Shops in Geylang, 1962. The heyday of Geylang Serai was in the1950s when it was a hub of shops, cinemas, hotels, the Great Eastern Trade Fair, and the Changi and Joo Chiat markets.

Its face changed in the 1960s, but not its significance. The first HDB project in the east raised Geylang Serai Market and the familar low-rise Blocks 4 and 5.

LEFT: Textile shop in Chinatown, 1962. Trebalco cotton of all colours and designs were available from such shops or from salesmen showing fabric swatches and taking orders from clients' homes.

ABOVE: Women sewing, 1962. Clothes were homemade or, if one could afford it, made-to-measure at tailors. Ethnic costumes were daily dress: samfoo, sari, sarong and dhoti.

OVERLEAF LEFT: Hock Lam Street, 1962.

Its shophouses, where multi-generational families lived on the upper floors and hung their laundry, framed the iconic tower of the Hill Street Fire Station.

The piping-hot bowls of delicious beef noodles served by a hawker here became well known as Hock Lam Street Beef Noodles.

OVERLEAF RIGHT: Bukit Merah Estate, 1963. In the 1950s, nine percent of the population lived in government-built flats. The Housing and Development Board, established in 1960, changed all that. By 1963, 20,000 flats were built, rising to 54,430 units by the time of Singapore's independence.

170

LEFT: A kampong in Alexandra Road, 1960s. The Urban Renewal Unit of the HDB was given responsibility in 1964 to transform such places by managing land use. This involved planning towns, building roads, providing transport infrastructure and piping clean water to homes.

RIGHT: Moving to a high-rise home, 1963. The HDB's rehousing programme was successful because it built flats quickly and was vested with the legal powers to resettle squatters.

Large families had to move a lifetime of possessions from kampong houses into smaller flats, many giving up livestock, farmland and friends. It was an uprooting of livelihood, lifestyle and community.

The HDB aimed to preserve the kampong spirit by designing precincts to 'encourage the spontaneous gathering of neighbours in an ambience of familiarity and togetherness.'

173

LEFT: Moving in, 1960s. Goodbye outhouse, kerosene lamps and well water. Hello modern sanitation, electricity and tap water.

Still, adjustments had to be made. After years of being at ground level, living in a highrise flat now meant operating lifts and having to buy your own vegetables, poultry and eggs.

RIGHT: Balloting for a flat, Commonwealth Drive, 1965. Ethnic integration – a key principle of flat allotment – ensured a good racial mix of occupants.

ABOVE: A new HDB home, 1965. Queenstown, first developed by the colonial Singapore Improvement Trust and then the HDB, is one of the oldest housing estates.

Completed in 1964, Blocks 74–80 Commonwealth Drive, with its 669 flats and 26 shops, were among the earliest HDB projects.

Popularly known as Tanglin Halt, its 10-storey blocks called Chap Lau Chu (10-storey houses) in Hokkien were featured on the back of Singapore's first dollar bill issued in 1967.

LEFT: Market Street multi-storey carpark, 1965. Singapore's first multi-floored carpark, the eight-storey Market Street Car Park opened in 1964 at the junction of Cross Street and Cecil Street. It had 780 parking lots for cars and 130 for motorcycles.

ABOVE: Driving test, 1950s. Singapore's only driving test centre was at the Maxwell Road Police Headquarters till another opened in Queenstown in 1968. There were 200,000 motor vehicles on the road in 1965, with some 80 new vehicles added every day.

OVERLEAF TOP LEFT: Raffles Place, 1962. Commercial Square, with its fenced garden in the centre, was renamed Raffles Place in 1858. In the 1920s, the garden was levelled to make a carpark and rickshaw station.

OVERLEAF BOTTOM LEFT: East Coast Road, 1965. The Singapore Improvement Trust master plan, implemented in 1958, introduced a hierarchy of arterial roads, radial routes, local roads, then access and minor roads. By the 1960s, metalled roads had reached the rural areas.

OVERLEAF TOP RIGHT: Road Safety First Playground, Kallang Park, 1960s. Over 30,000 students from 200 schools and about 1,000 members of the public visited in 1961, the year it opened. This was the venue of the Shell Traffic Games.

OVERLEAF BOTTOM RIGHT: Collyer Quay, 1962. The first pedestrian bridge was built here next to Clifford Pier in 1964. Fullerton Building was from where road distances were measured. Hence, 7 milestone Bukit Timah Road and 5½ milestone Changi Road.

PREVIOUS: New Bridge Road, 1962. The landmarks on the road then were Majestic Theatre and Pearl's Market. The cinema, owned by Cathay Organisation since 1956, reached its height of popularity in the 1950s and 60s. The open-air stalls, also known as People's Park Market, were burnt down on Christmas eve 1966.

ABOVE: Quayside, 1960s. The Singapore River in 1959 was a centre of commerce and handled a similar volume of goods as Keppel Harbour. It remained an important economic area into the 1960s.

RIGHT: Pepper warehouse, Tanjong Pagar, 1960. Rubber, coffee, palm oil and pepper led Singapore exports in the 1960s.

Pythons were known to be kept in some warehouses that stored agricultural products to control the infestation of rats.

LEFT: Worker and *jaga* (watchman) of a textile mill, Bukit Timah, 1963. One of the few industrial operations in the early 1960s, the mill was run by a Shanghainese entrepreneur. Locked out by strikes, the owner turned it into a factory making steel windows.

RIGHT: Coffee shop boy, 1962. The 14-hour work day started at 5 am for *kopi kia* or coffee shop boys. The job was not just about taking and shouting orders, but being a general dogsbody, including scrubbing toilets, emptying spittoons – and dealing with gangsters.

LEFT: Chinatown shophouse, 1960s. Some 250,000 people lived in century-old buildings in the city.

RIGHT & BELOW: Death in Chinatown, 1960s. Funerals, with bands, ornate hearses and sackcloth-clad mourners were common. Chinese hardwood caskets made in Pickering Street or Coffin Street were sealed according to ritual.

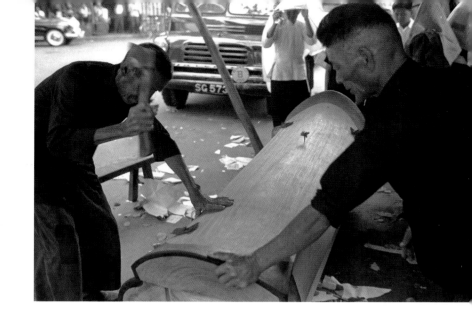

LEFT: Funeral of Josephine Cornelius, Bidadari Cemetery, 1961.

ABOVE: Chinese graveyard, 1960.

In 1960, the crude death rate, which is the number of deaths occurring per 1,000 population during the year was 6.20.

After independence, because of improved living standards, better healthcare policies and higher levels of medical care, the number fell significantly to 5.40. The top two causes of death were tuberculosis and pneumonia.

OVERLEAF: Fish ponds in Alexandra, 1961. Such inland fisheries primarily reared five species of carp: Grass, Big head, Mud, Silver and the Common Carp, with each species having a part in the eco-system of the ponds.

In 1949, there were about 121 hectares of fish ponds. The First Five Year Plan for land use of 1961–1965 sought to increase the area given to fish breeding by another 800 hectares.

ABOVE: Vegetable farm, Potong Pasir, 1962.

BELOW: Sorting fruit, Tanjong Kling, Jurong, c 1959.

RIGHT: Farmers at work, 1960.

The Primary Production Department was formed in 1959 to improve food production by introducing new methods of farming and fishing. Books on the rearing of tilapia fish and goats were published in 1963 and 1965 respectively.

Mud dykes formed prawn ponds at estuaries or mangrove swamps. Open sluice gates allowed prawns and small fish to be carried in with the tide, and when the water receded, nets trapped the seafood as water flowed through the gates.

ABOVE: Serangoon Gardens, 1963. Flower gardens and farms which replaced rubber estates in the post-war period gave the area its name. Private landed houses built there ranged from $12,000 for a terrace house to $21,000 for a bungalow.

LEFT: Poultry farm, 1962. Singapore was then an exporter of eggs. The number of chickens in the 1960s was 20 times more than the human population.

BELOW: Kampong telephone booth, 1960s. Public phones away from the city were rare up to the 1960s. In the late 50s, one public phone served 6,500 residents in Sembawang Hills Estate.

OVERLEAF TOP LEFT: Firing crackers, Nee Soon, 1963. Crackers were fired to celebrate festivals, but were also set off by Chinese communities to ward off bad luck.

OVERLEAF BOTTOM LEFT: Barongan and Kuda Kepang procession, Bukit Panjang, 1965. These folk dances, which could involve trances, were performed at weddings and other Malay celebrations.

OVERLEAF RIGHT: Malay wedding, 1960. The bride and groom carried in procession to the solemnisation ceremony.

TOP LEFT: Street opera, 1960. *Wayang* shows performed on makeshift wooden stages moved from venue to venue but were always accompanied by food stalls and hawkers selling toys, offering a multi-sensory treat for both the young and old.

BOTTOM LEFT: Sin Wah Theatre, Bukit Panjang, 1960s. Other cinemas in the suburbs included Roxy (East Coast), Kok Wah (Yio Chu Kang), New City (Aljunied), Paramount (Serangoon), Queens (Geylang) and Taj (Changi). City-centre choices were Capitol, Cathay, Lido, New Alhambra, Odeon, Jubilee, Majestic and Rex cinemas.

ABOVE: *Wayang* troupe backstage, 1963. Street opera declined in the 1950s and 60s due to the depressed economy, social and political unrest, and the rise of television.

FACING: National Theatre, 1960s. Built on the slopes of Fort Canning Hill off Clemenceau Avenue, the 3,420-seat, $2.2-million building was completed in 1964 (although the partially finished theatre was used to open the inaugural Southeast Asia Cultural Festival on 8 August 1963). Designed by architect Alfred Wong, its iconic facade featured five vertical diamond-shaped bays.

ABOVE: School concert, 1962.

RIGHT: A multi-racial audience, 1963. Singapore's multiracialism was formally recognised in the 1950s, crystalising into the Chinese, Indian, Malay and Others (CIMO) model in the post-independence years. Still, the national pledge declares that Singaporeans are one people regardless of race.

PREVIOUS: HDB housing, 1965. By mid-1965, the HDB had exceeded its target set in its first 5-year plan of 1960, housing a quarter of Singapore's population in 51,000 apartment units.

TOP LEFT: Tree planting, Alexandra, 1964. By the end of the 1950s, the government's post-war tree-planting programme resulted in the greening of residential areas but less so the business district.

Another campaign, in 1963, to plant 10,000 new trees each year, was initially unsuccessful. The reason: people's lack of empathy for trees and a lack of expertise.

BOTTOM LEFT: Building works, 1960s. Accelerated development provided regular work to *samsui* women whom the British called 'Concrete Lizzies'.

ABOVE: Block 104 Commonwealth Crescent and site office, 1963.

RIGHT: View from Kallang Gasworks, 1964. United Nations representatives, invited in 1962 and 1963 to help formulate a long-term urban development plan, take in the cityscape.

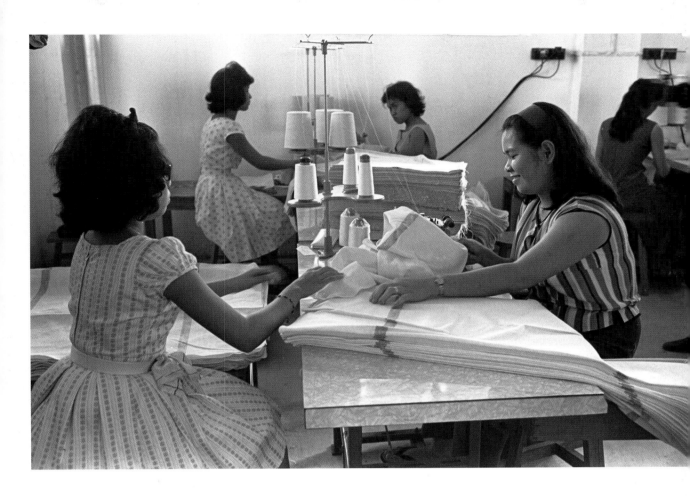

LEFT: Rubber smokehouse, 1950s. There were once 15 rubber factories in Singapore. They included mills to clean the rubber, and smokehouses to extract moisture from the material.

ABOVE: Union Textile, Kampong Ampat, 1964. Garment factories undertook contract sewing jobs – cut, make and trim – or the full-package for Singapore and overseas clients.

RIGHT: Government Printing Office, 1963. The press printed everything for official use, from gazettes, exam papers, reports and forms to posters and invitation cards.

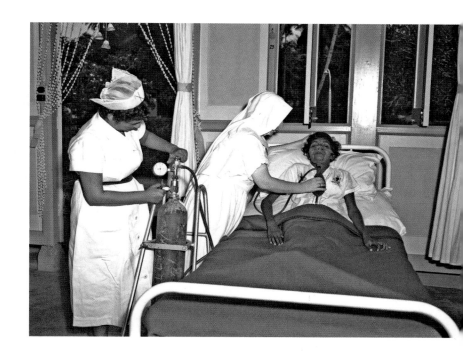

LEFT: Chinese medical hall, 1962. Well into the 1960s, healthcare was rudimentary, and the different races relied on traditional medical treatments which used herbs, minerals, animal parts and oils as cures.

By 1960, a training school for Chinese physicians had functioned for seven years, and Eu Yan Sang medical hall had rendered service for half a century.

ABOVE: Mandalay Road Hospital, 1959. On attaining self-government, priority was given to defence, housing and education. Healthcare was perhaps sixth down the line.

Yet, there existed nursing training, a medical school and public, private and missionary hospitals practising Western medicine. Think Tan Tock Seng, St Andrew's Mission and Singapore General at Sepoy Lines.

ABOVE LEFT: In a garden in Siglap, 1961.

ABOVE RIGHT: Girl with an Indian milkman's calf, Winstead Road flats, 1961.

RIGHT: On the famous tembusu tree, Botanic Gardens, c 1962.

FACING: Horsing around during a graduation portrait session, Botanic Gardens, 1964.

ABOVE: A tea party in a home in Bukit Timah, 1950s.

LEFT: On a HDB balcony, 1964.

TOP RIGHT: Celebrating baby's first month, 1963.

RIGHT: Friends in a backlane, 1963.

Simple rhythms of life, familial connections, friendships forged at home and in common spaces.

ABOVE: On the French liner, SS *Cambridge,* 1963.

RIGHT: Farewell at Keppel Harbour, 1962.

For most visitors, before air travel became affordable, the first and last sight of Singapore – a maritime hub linking Europe via the Suez Canal to the Far East – was from the sea glimpsed through the green islets south of the harbour.

OVERLEAF: Flooded homes, 1963. Floods were the result of poor drainage and heavy rain coinciding with the onset of high tides.

The widening of drains, the building of tidal gates and the raising of low-lying areas in the 1960s helped to prevent flooding in Queenstown, Geylang, Bedok, Potong Pasir and Whampoa. But, ironically, flooding intensified with the increased surface runoff from the development of housing and industrial estates.

LEFT: River Valley Swimming Complex, 1963. These Olympic-sized and wading pools, which cost $520,000 to build, were located in King George V Park at the foot of Fort Canning Hill.

Opened in 1959, it augmented public pools in Yan Kit Road and Farrer Park, which operated from 1952 and 1957 respectively.

Swimming as a recreational activity increased in popularity in the 1960s when it was promoted because it was seen as a social leveler.

ABOVE: Human pyramid, RAF Seletar, 1959. Joint Air Traffic Control Centre staff enjoy the camp pool that was mainly used for aircrew dingy training in the largest British Royal Air Force (RAF) base in the Far East. The pool was upgraded in 1963 using funds raised at a fete in 1961.

Other private club pools in Singapore included the YMCA pool on Fort Canning Hill (1919), Chinese Swimming Club (1905), Britannia Club's olympic-sized Nuffield Pool (1951) and the Royal Island Club pool (1957).

BELOW: Art exhibition, Victoria Memorial Hall, 1960. Abdul Ghani Hamid, president of Angkatan Pelukis Aneka Daya (Association of Artists of Various Resources) and Lim Yew Kwan, second principal of Nanyang Fine Arts College, at the first exhibition of Malay artists.

RIGHT: Artist and sculptures, 1960. The busts of Lee Kuan Yew and Tunku Abdul Rahman with their sculptor, Ong Keng Wee, the father of Ong Teng Cheong.

Preparing a tea reception,
Punggol, 1963.
Restaurants and caterers
brought everything,
including the kitchen
sink, on site to serve food
cooked á la minute.

PREVIOUS: Setting up a group photograph, 1963. Members of the Lim clan pose at their association house, Sai Ho Piat Su, in Upper Serangoon Road. The location was unusual, as most clubhouses of Chinese groups were clustered in Chinatown and the Beach Road area.

LEFT: Family portrait, 1960. In the late 1950s, 22 percent of households had 'more than one family nucleus', that is, they were extended families.

BELOW: Mandalay Villa, Katong, 1959. This imposing bungalow at 29 Amber Road was the home of Mrs Lee Choon Guan in the 1950s and 60s.

The house had 13 rooms. It also had a pavilion built over the sea with a living room and two bedrooms gilded by Italian artists.

The expansive grounds with a rose garden and fountain were the main venue for parties organised by the matriarch.

229

PREVIOUS: Houses and a shop, Joo Chiat, 1964. These images, part of a survey conducted by the Public Works Department, show the types of residential and commercial buildings of the day in Katong.

FACING: Picture-perfect kampong, 1960s. The idea of kampongs being seaside Malay villages is a misleading stereotype. Chinese, Indian, Malay and multi-racial kampongs were dotted all over Singapore, from Kampong Cantek Bahru at the foot of Bukit Timah, Bulim Village in Jurong, Kampong Saigon on the Singapore River, and Kampong O'Carroll Scott in Buona Vista.

TOP: At a World War II pillbox in Labrador, 1965.

LEFT: Beach scenes, 1960s. Changi Beach was a popular place to swim and picnic. Stretching from the spit at Changi Creek to the cliffs of Tanah Merah Besar, it was lined with sea almond, coconut and casuarina trees under which shacks and vans offered *satay*, *vadai* and chips. There, one could also hire deck chairs, sampans and inner tubes.

ABOVE AND BELOW: Boat races, c 1963. Boat racing was popular among the Malay kampongs of Katong, Siglap, Pasir Panjang, and Pulau Tekong. Kampong pride would be at stake as adults and children raced their *kolek* and the model-sized *jong* against the boats of other kampongs.

RIGHT: Seletar Yacht Club, 1959. The crew of the Sutherland Flying Boats, as well as nautically-inclined servicemen based at RAF Seletar, treated the yacht club like their crew room, relaxing on the veranda, enjoying club sandwiches and beer.

Other sailing clubs then were the Singapore Yacht Club in Pasir Panjang and the Royal Air Force Yacht Club in Changi.

OVERLEAF: Katong Beach, 1962. Chinese fishing villages dotted East Coast Road while villages of Malay fishermen clustered around Changi and Pulau Tekong. Of the estimated 5,000 who fished for a living, a third were Malay, and two-thirds were Chinese. There were only about six Indian fishermen in total.

TOP: Land reclamation, Bedok, 1962. Some 19.5 hectares were reclaimed at Bedok as part of a pilot project. Its success prompted the reclaiming of 400 hectares from Tanjong Rhu to Bedok from 1966.

ABOVE: Cycling along hilly terrain, c 1963. In the 1960s, the hills from Mount Faber to Pasir Panjang, Jurong to Sarimboon and the foothills of Bukit Timah were not yet encroached upon. The Gap, since renamed Kent Ridge, with its numerous turns, was a popular cycling and motoring route from the mid-1920s.

RIGHT: MacRitchie Reservoir, 1963. Completed in 1868, the reservoir was renamed in 1922 after the Municipal Engineer James Mac-Ritchie. The reservoir park opened in 1967 and soon became popular with strollers, joggers and lovers.

ABOVE: Captain's ball, Primary Production Department Veterinary Training School, Sembawang, 1960s. A Farm School was also opened by the department in 1965, taking in students with a minimum of primary six education who were full-time farmers or were the wards of one.

RIGHT: Katong Park, 1965. The park, built in the 1930s over the buried Fort Tanjong Katong, had a splendid seaview, bathing *pagar* and food hawkers, making it an attractive place for family activities.

In 1959, it was chosen as the venue of an Aneka Ragam Ra'ayat (People's Cultural Concert).

Three bombs were set off at the popular park in September and October 1963 during the Indonesian Konfrontasi.

OVERLEAF: Rugby game, Padang, 1964. The All Blues, a team comprising exclusively of civilian players, represented Singapore in the Federated States of Malaya matches from the early 1900s. This team would later become the Singapore Civilians Team that played in the Malaya Cup competitions until independence in 1965.

ALL ON THIS SPREAD: Queen Elizabeth Walk, 1960s. The seafront promenade was officially named and opened on 30 May 1953 by Lady Yuen-Peng McNeice, wife of the first president of Singapore's City Council, Sir Percy McNeice.

That esplanade, which had been long known to the Chinese as 'Goh Chang Chiew Kah' (under the five trees), was popular for evening strolls to catch the sea breeze, with dinner afterwards at hawkers parked there.

OVERLEAF: Hockey match at dusk, Padang, 1962.

TOP: Fishing with a
push net, Katong, 1962.

ABOVE: Twilight on
Merdeka Bridge, 1962.
The three-lane,
610-metre structure
connected the east coast
and the city across the
Kallang Basin. The
bridge, guarded by a
pair of lions crafted
by the Italian sculptor
Rodolfo Nolli, was
officially opened in
August 1956.

RIGHT: Beo Crescent
Market, 1965. Opened
on 19 April that year, it
had been built on the site
of the devastating fire that
engulfed the kampongs
of Bukit Ho Swee on
the afternoon of 25
May 1961. Over 16,000
people lost their homes
but just nine months later
they were moved into
'emergency one-room
flats' in Jalan Bukit Ho
Swee.

LEFT: Breaking fast, 1960. Unlike the Chinese and Indian populations, Malays were concentrated outside the city core, living mainly in Geylang Serai and Jalan Eunos, with small, loose communities found on the periphery of Pasir Panjang, Changi, south Jurong and the Southern Islands.

BELOW: Koran reading contest, 1963. The Administration of Muslim Law Bill, which was passed in 1960, formed a council of Muslim affairs. By then, Singapore had some 14 mosques.

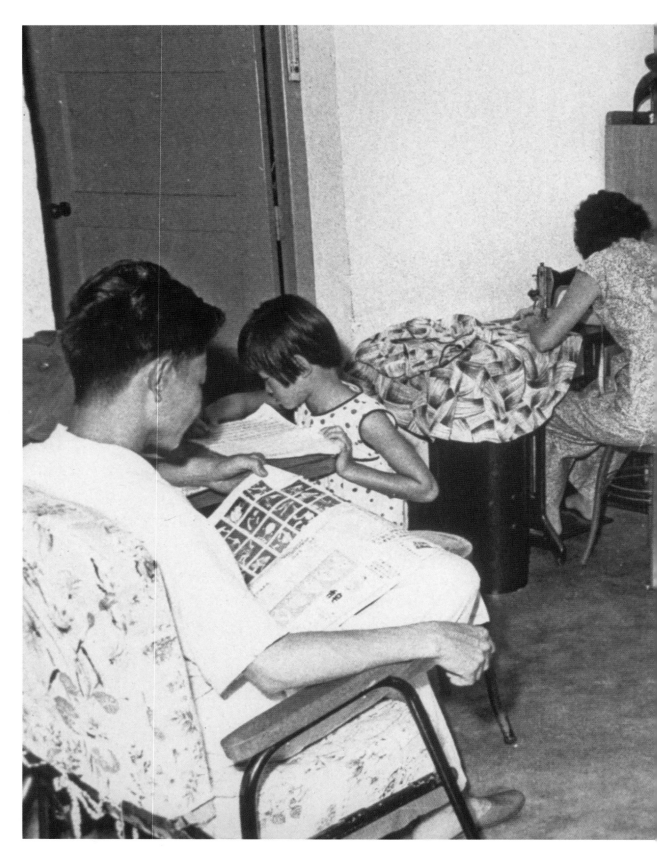

PREVIOUS: In a HDB living room, 1960s.

ABOVE: Eating durians before bedtime, Chancery Lane, c 1960.

RIGHT: An amah preparing dinner for her employer's family, Chancery Lane, c 1960.

TOP FACING: A Eurasian family plays chess, Bendemeer, 1960s.

BOTTOM FACING: Prelude to a pillow fight, Upper Serangoon, 1963.

Settlement patterns shifted in the 1950s and 60s as social conditions changed. As British military housing decentralised, so did the population that served the soldiers and their families.

The rapid growth of a middle class and the introduction of private estates and government–built flats created the suburbs.

Still, in 1966, the population in the core of the city was 1.2 million, meaning 61 percent of the people lived in 16 percent of the area of Singapore.

LEFT: The Cresendos on set, 1963.

ABOVE: Recording an Aneka Ragam Ra'ayat community concert, 1963.

Television arrived on 15 February 1963, broadcasting from 7.15 pm to 11.15 pm in the four official languages on the single channel of Television Singapura.

Pioneer variety productions featured Singapore talent such as the crossover Rediffusion storyteller Lee Dai Soh, and The Cresendos comprising Susan Lim, John Chee, Raymond Ho and Leslie Chia.

Only one in 58 families had TVs then, but the increase was fast enough for Setron – Singapore Electronics – to begin assembling sets at its factory at Tanglin Halt in late 1964.

OVERLEAF: Storyteller by the Singapore River, 1960. Before the rise of television, illiterate labourers, trishaw pullers and hawkers gathered at night and paid to hear folktales and stories from ancient history and martial arts novels. These were read by storytellers of different dialect groups in different locations: Teochew in Boat Quay, Hokkien in Telok Ayer and Cantonese off South Bridge Road.

LEFT: Entrance to New World park, 1962.

ABOVE: Great World amusement park, 1962.

RIGHT: Agricultural show, Kallang Park, 1965.

Entrance to the worlds of entertainment – New World, Great World, Happy World, Gay World – cost pocket change. And from dusk to midnight, a myriad of activities for every taste (all ticketed separately) were on offer: Chinese opera and *bangsawan* theatre, cinemas, fairground rides, circus acts, cabarets, dancing girls, even striptease shows.

These glittering amusement parks, supported by food stalls, restaurants, shops selling everything from toys to textiles, and trade exhibitions too, began to fade in the 1960s.

The death blows were delivered by television and the emerging shopping malls. Great World, for example, shuttered every attraction, except its cinemas and restaurants, in 1964.

PREVIOUS: City street lights of North Bridge Road, 1964. Neon signs gave colour and movement to the streetscape. Older people may recall the giant, glowing bottle of soy sauce at Bukit Timah Circus, the National Showroom Tower by Capitol Cinema, and the animated ad for ENO Fruit Salt above Newton Post Office.

ABOVE: Basketball match, 1961. Singapore gained its strong position in regional basketball when teams played in the Asian Basketball Cup and the 1956 Melbourne Olympic Games. This boosted amateur basketball in schools of every language stream and also in community centres.

RIGHT: Wrestling at a sports centre, 1959. Amusment parks promoted wrestling, with exhibition matches by the likes of Tiger Ahmad and King Kong.

Boxing was popular too, as much as football, with boys' clubs and schools like St Joseph's and St Andrew's offering the sport.

FACING TOP: Dinner and Dance, Queenstown, 1964. These dancers are doing the twist, the worldwide dance craze from 1959 to the early 60s.

In 1959, the government clamped down on 'yellow-culture' – aspects of Western pop culture seen to promote a decadent or antisocial lifestyle. In one fell swoop, juke boxes, pin-table saloons and striptease shows were outlawed.

FACING BOTTOM: Dance girls, 1964. Popular dance halls employed 100 taxi dancers or more, mostly locals with some from China, Thailand and the Philippines.

The price was a dollar for three dances – Malay *ronggeng* and *joget* or Western styles – redeemed by pre-paid coupons.

LEFT: Singer at a Khek community guild dinner, 1959. The difference between traditional songs and popular songs summarises the polar opposites in Chinese music then. Those who encouraged the development of popular tunes sung in *getai* were considered 'unscrupulous, immoral and socially irresponsible' by traditionalists.

BELOW: Fairground outside a cabaret, 1964. A thriving nightlife revolved around cabarets with names like Shangri-la, Bunga Tanjong, Broadway and Man Jiang Hong Getai.

PREVIOUS LEFT: Community event, Jalan Hwi Yoh, 1964.

PREVIOUS RIGHT: Chinese puppetry, 1963.

LEFT: National Theatre, 1963. The theatre, built with donations raised from the public through 'a-dollar-a-brick' campaign and government funds, had a 150-tonne cantilevered steel roof which reached towards the slopes of Fort Canning Hill.

RIGHT: Dressing room, Happy World, 1963. A Hong Kong Cantonese opera troupe, including star Sun Ma Chai, performed to raise funds for the National Theatre.

BELOW: Aneka Ragam Ra'ayat (People's Cultural Concert), 1960. Cultural performances were once confined to the festive and religious celebrations of each race. In 1959, a series of free, open-air Aneka Ragam Ra'ayat organised by the Ministry of Culture featured a multi-racial programme.

LEFT: Queenstown Community Centre, 1962. Some 60 community centres were opened in 1961. Managed by the People's Association, the centres disseminated government information and policies, as well as received feedback. Activities, from cooking classes to sewing lessons were organised to promote social unity while games were hosted to take loitering youth off the streets.

ABOVE: Dance performance, Queenstown Community Centre, 1962. Residents get-together sessions featuring multi-racial items were held to promote harmony and national identity among the various races.

FAR LEFT: Weightlifting competition, Kallang Community Centre, 1965. Tan Howe Liang's silver medal for lightweight weightlifting at the 1960 Rome Olympics – Singapore's first Olympic medal – inspired aspiring Singaporean strongmen.

LEFT: Dr Goh Keng Swee at a meet-the-people session, 1961.

PREVIOUS & THIS SPREAD: Pasar Malam in Chinatown, 1960s. Weekly night markets, timed according to the pay day of servicemen, started in the mid-1950s near British military bases at Seletar and Sembawang.

Also known as night bazaars, these spread to public and private housing estates in the 1960s and were welcomed by residents for bringing goods to their doorsteps as shops then were found mainly in the city centre.

Hawkers offering finger food and street stalls selling goods from toys and footwear to haberdashery and household goods moved to different locations in a fixed circuit. Some 40 night markets operated weekly.

ABOVE: Birthday party, 1960. Many would have blown candles off on a cream cake probably bought from Mont D'or, Balmoral Bakery, Red House or Cold Storage Creameries. Other delights also served were cream horns, swan-shaped cream puffs, chocolate rum balls and Swiss rolls.

LEFT: Leaving party, 1959. The non-Asian business and military populations in Singapore were transient, returning home after each tour of duty. Thus, leaving parties were held regularly where guests presented their departing friends with curios and Eastern souvenirs as mementoes of their time spent in the Far Eastern port.

RIGHT: Mrs Lee Choon Guan's birthday dinner, Mandalay Villa, 1959. Her guests, which included prominent personalities and Malay royalty, mingled in the grounds of her Katong seaside villa.

Meanwhile, the fisherfolk of Kampong Amber paraded to express their felicitation and show their appreciation for being allowed to live rent-free on her land.

ABOVE: At a dance championship, Raffles Hotel, 1963.

RIGHT: Tea Dance, 1959.

LEFT: One, Two, Cha Cha Cha, 1963.

Dancing was part of the social life of Europeans and Asians alike. Tea dances were held mainly on Sunday afternoons with a cover charge of $3, including cakes and drinks.

Into the 1960s, the cha cha, foxtrot and waltz gave way to the twist and the shake. New venues like Cellar on Collyer Quay, and Golden Venus and Prince's Hotel Garni along Orchard Road overtook the dance floors of Raffles, Adelphi and Sea View.

PREVIOUS: Durian stall, Queen Street, 1962. Durians were kampong grown, with an estimated 60,000 durian trees in Singapore in the 1960s.

ABOVE, LEFT & RIGHT: Bugis Street, 1962. It was a tourist ghetto where alcohol and food (including dishes of frogs and snakes) were not the only things enjoyed in excess every night. Bugis Street was also famous for its strutting, stripping transvestites, and raucous sailors dancing on the roof of a public toilet with cigars of burning newspapers gripped between their bare bottoms.

OVERLEAF: Mahjong at a death house, Sago Lane, 1962. Amahs and friends occupy time at a wake.

LAST SPREAD: Late at night, a street stall awaits customers looking for supper, 1962.

PICTURE CREDITS

National Archives of Singapore
Pages 10 (top right and middle right, bottom middle), 17, 33, 34-35, 37 (top and bottom), 32, 40, 47 (right), 50, 51, 70, 71, 74 (bottom), 75, 76-77, 78 (top), 79 (bottom), 80-81, 82 (bottom), 83, 84 (top and bottom), 86-87, 88, 89, 91 (top), 92-93, 94 (bottom), 95 (top and bottom), 98, 99 (top), 100-101, 102 (bottom), 103, 105 (top), 106-107, 111, 112-113, 115, 120, 121 (top and bottom), 122-123, 124 (top and bottom), 130-131, 132 (top and bottom), 133, 134, 135 (top), 146 (top), 148, 160 (top), 161 (bottom), 163 (top and bottom), 165, 167 (right), 168, 170, 179 (bottom), 180-181, 183, 185, 187 (top and bottom), 192 (top), 192-193, 197, 198 (top left), 205 (top), 208-209, 226, 227, 231 (bottom), 234-235, 236 (top left), 236-237, 242 (bottom), 244-245, 246 (top and bottom), 256-257, 258, 259 (top), 265 (top), 267, 272-273, 275 (top), 277, 278 (top), 280-281, 282 (top), 283, 284-285 and 286-287. A J Hawker Collection, page 147. Abdul Ghani Hamid Collection, pages 220-221. ABN AMRO Art & History, Amsterdam Collection, page 178 (top). Aerial photographs by the British Royal Air Force between 1940 to 1970s, from a collection held by the National Archives of Singapore. Crown copyright, endpapers and pages 42 and 67. Arthur B Reich Collection, page 74 (top). David Ng Collection, pages 126-127, 140 (bottom) and 278 (top). Derek Lehrle Collection, pages 96-97. Eelke Wolters Collection, pages 146, 162, 172 and 236 (bottom left). George Tricker Collection, page 105 (bottom). George W Porter Collection, pages 6-7 and 182. Ho Chin Geok Collection, pages 10 (top middle) and 63. Jack Sim Collection, pages 125 (top) and 145 (right). Kau Luen Tong Sze-To Clan Guild Collection, page 189 (top right). Lim Kim San Collection, pages 278-279. Majlis Ugama Islam Singapura Collection, page 248. Margaret Clarke Collection, pages 188-189, 212 (top), 231 (middle) and 253 (top). Marine Parade Community Centre Collection, pages 38-39. Martha Scully-Shepherdson Collection, page 10 (bottom right). Ministry of Culture Collection, pages 79 (top), 94 (top), 137 and 204 (bottom). Ministry of Information and the Arts Collection, pages front cover, back cover (left and right), spine, 4-5, 10 (middle left), 12, 14, 15, 18, 19, 20, 21, 23, 25 (top and bottom), 27, 28, 29, 43 (bottom), 44, 46-47, 48-49, 50 (top), 54 (top), 54-55, 55 (right), 56, 57 (top), 59 (bottom), 60-61, 62 (top), 68-69, 72, 73, 78 (bottom), 90-91, 102 (top), 104, 108, 109 (top and bottom), 110 (top and bottom), 114 (top), 116-117, 118 (top and bottom), 119, 125 (bottom), 128 (top and bottom), 129 (top and bottom), 135 (bottom), 136-137, 138, 139 (top and bottom), 140 (top), 141, 142-143, 144-145, 149 (top and bottom), 152, 153 (top and bottom), 154-155, 156 (top), 157, 161 (top), 164 (top and bottom), 166-167, 169, 171, 173, 175 (top and bottom), 176, 177, 178 (bottom), 179 (top), 184, 186, 190-191, 194 (top), 195, 196 (top and bottom), 198 (bottom left), 198-199, 201 (top and bottom), 202-203, 204 (top), 205 (bottom), 206, 207 (top and bottom), 209, 212 (bottom), 213 (bottom), 214 (left), 216-217, 218-219, 222-223, 224-225, 228 (top and bottom), 229 (top and bottom), 230, 232 (top), 239, 240-241, 242 (top), 243, 246-247, 249 (right), 250-251, 254-255, 259 (right), 260-261, 262, 263, 264 (top and bottom), 265 (bottom), 266, 268, 269 (top and bottom), 270 (top and bottom), 271 (top and bottom), 274, 275 (bottom) and 282 (bottom). Mr & Mrs Chua Thor Cheng Collection, page 194 (bottom). Nachiappa Chettiar Collection, page 91 (bottom). National Museum of Singapore Collection, page 36. Nelson Collection, pages 2-3. Ong Teng Cheong Collection, page 221 (top). People's Association Collection, page 174. Primary Production Department Collection, pages 41, 43 (top), 45 (top and bottom), 52-53, 238 and 259 (bottom). RAFSA Collection, pages 10 (bottom left), 64 (top and bottom), 65 (all), 66, 99 (bottom), 219 (right) and 232-233. S Rajaratnam Collection, page 276 (top). School of Nursing Collection, page 58. Tampines Primary School Collection, pages 62 (bottom), 63 (top), 114 (bottom) and 150-151. The Ralph Charles Saunders Collection, pages 57 (bottom) and 276 (bottom). The Trekkers Collection, page 22. Urban Redevelopment Authority Collection, pages 158-159. William Teo Jui Wah Collection, back cover (middle) and page 200.

Photographs taken by K.F. Wong (National Archives of Singapore collection), pages 10 (bottom middle), 33, 34-35, 37 (top and bottom), 32, 40, 70, 71, 74 (bottom), 75, 76-77, 78 (top), 79 (bottom), 80-81, 83, 84 (top and bottom), 86-87, 88, 89, 91 (top), 92-93, 94 (bottom), 95 (top and bottom), 99, 100-101, 102 (bottom), 103, 105 (top), 106-107, 111, 112-113, 121 (top and bottom), 122-123, 124 (top and bottom), 130-131, 132 (top and bottom), 134, 135 (top), 146 (top), 160 (top), 161 (bottom), 163 (top and bottom), 165, 167 (right), 168, 170, 179 (bottom), 180-181, 183, 185, 187 (top and bottom), 192 (top), 192-193, 208-209, 227, 231 (bottom), 234-235, 236 (top left), 236-237, 242 (bottom), 244-245, 246 (top and bottom), 256-257, 258, 259 (top), 267, 272-273, 275 (top), 277, 280-281, 282 (top), 283, 284-285 and 286-287.

From the Family and Friends: A Singapore Album (2008), a project co-organised by Nexus, National Museum of Singapore and Landmark Books Bernice Lau Kai Qing Collection, page 59 (top). Chia Ming Chien Collection, page 253 (bottom). Frederick Koh Collection, page 192 (bottom). Jimmy Lye Kwok Poo Collection, pages 231 (top) and 232 bottom. K Chandra Collection, page 85 (top). Katherine Seow Collection, page 210 (top left). Lau Nyeng Siang Collection, page 210 (top right). Law Yong Siang Collection, page 210 (bottom). Lee Geok Boi Collection, pages 16, 24 and 26. Mun Chor Weng Collection, page 211. Nicole Lim Si Min Collection, page 213 (top). P Siva Collection, page 85 (bottom). Xener Kaur Gill Collection, page 82 (top).

Private Collections
Goh Eck Kheng, pages 10 (top left), 214-215. Sharon Ong, pages 156 (bottom), 160 (bottom) and 252 (both).